7 MINUTE COVER LETTERS

DANA MORGAN

IDG Books Worldwide, Inc.
An International Data Group Company
Foster City, CA • Chicago, IL • Indianapolis, IN • New York, NY

1st Edition

IDG Books Worldwide, Inc.
An International Data Group Company
919 E. Hillsdale Boulevard
Suite 400
Foster City, CA 94404

An ARCO Book

For general information on IDG Books Worldwide's books in the U.S., please call our Consumer Customer Service department at 800-762-2974. For reseller information, including discounts and premium sales, please call our Reseller Customer Service department at 800-434-3422.

Library of Congress information available on request

ISBN: 0-7645-6082-4

Manufactured in the United States of America

10 9 8 7 6 5 4 3 2 1

TABLE OF CONTENTS

ACKNOWLEDGMENTS

To Joel: for remaining calm and steady in the midst of widespread upheaval.

To Kiera, Taylor, Chase, and Garrick: for their patience and fun-loving spirits.

To my parents: without whose constant assistance I couldn't have written this book.

To Grandma and Grandpa Morgan: who selflessly provided help and support.

To Lisa Ruffalo, Debbie Ostrowski, Sally Campbell, and all the professionals at Manchester Partners International: who join me in the mission to find great jobs for great people.

To all the hard-working job seekers that I have had the pleasure to work with: May you all achieve great success in your exciting career adventures!

Introduction

John Q. Hiring Manager sits at his desk at 11:00 A.M. In front of him is a stack of morning mail as tall as the picture of his dog Fido that adorns his desk. In that stack, among all the other job hopefuls, is an envelope containing your cover letter and resume. It is firmly entrenched somewhere in the middle of the pile, looking from the outside much like all the other envelopes waiting to be opened.

John Q. Hiring Manager finally takes his stainless-steel letter opener and slices open your envelope. The first thing he sees, placed attractively atop your resume, is your cover letter. Because he's having a busy morning, he gives your cover letter only about 10 seconds of his attention.

This is your moment of truth. What are you going to say in those 10 seconds that will impress him—entice him—persuade him that you have what it takes to do the job? Whatever it is, it has to be good. This is the opportunity you've been waiting for. This may be your only chance to capture his attention.

Cover letters are notorious for eliciting groans from job seekers who pale at the thought of writing a letter that will be scrutinized by hiring managers with the power to make or break their career. The cover letter adds major stress to an already stressful job search process.

Writing cover letters doesn't have to be as awful as all that, though. This book is designed specifically to take the pain out of the writing process and to make your cover letter work for you. A well-written cover letter can actually open doors for you that might otherwise remain firmly shut.

So let's get busy! Together we can create a cover letter that will breathe life into your job search and smoothly escort your resume into the hands of the employers you want to impress.

CHAPTER 1

Understanding the Cover Letter's Purpose and Audience

In this chapter, you will learn how cover letters fit into your job campaign, and how a well-crafted cover letter can enhance the power of your resume. You also will learn what hiring managers are looking for when they read your letter.

THE COVER LETTER DEFINED

Job seekers of the past tended to view cover letters as a necessary evil in the job search process. Most cover letter writers were content to dash off a quick note that said little more than, "Thanks for reading my resume." This old-fashioned school of thought failed to recognize the great opportunity that cover letters offer.

Today's cover letter fulfills a grander purpose than to politely preface the resume; cover letters are now used as a way to *enhance* the resume.

Well-crafted cover letters add credibility to the resume, strengthen its claims, and present a personal dimension that the resume alone can't convey.

As you begin your job search campaign, you may assume that one generalized cover letter will fill the need in all of your job search situations. This is not quite true, since you will be exposed to many different situations throughout your job search that will require different types of responses. Each cover letter type will be discussed in detail in later chapters, but in general a cover letter serves as a bridge between your resume and the person who reads your resume. The letter points out details from the resume that are of particular interest to the hiring manager and demonstrates how your accomplishments in previous positions translate into a match for the skills the manager needs. Use your cover letter to capture the attention and the imagination of the reader so that he or she will want to learn more by reading your resume.

HOW A COVER LETTER ENHANCES YOUR RESUME

A well-crafted cover letter helps you get your message of success to the people with the power to hire you. Here are some ways a good cover letter can enhance your resume:

- **Highlights the positives** Here's your chance to highlight the skills, accomplishments, and achievements on your resume that you're particularly proud of. Glance over your resume a few times. What do you want to be sure the reader doesn't miss? These are the things to include in your cover letter!

- **Adds a personal touch to an otherwise generic document** A resume is, by definition, a standardized overview of your skills and background. It says very little about your personality or attitude, yet these attributes are just as important to hiring managers as job skills. Give them a sense of who you are in your cover letter and entice them to find out more about you.

- **Explains points of interest that are specific to that company or position** A cover letter should never seem like a rehash of an unimaginative and irrelevant general template. It should relate to that particular job and that particular company, and give your readers a taste of how you fit their specific needs. Use your cover letter as a bridge to link your skills and accomplishments to the company's current needs.

- **Offers insight into your job search situation**   It's helpful to clarify your job search situation in your cover letter, as long as it doesn't present negatives to your potential employers. If you are relocating to their geographic area, for example, make this clear in your letter, but leave out specifics on the time frame of your search or other parameters that may not fit with their needs.

The cover letter is not the place to bring up complicated employment issues that would be better explained in person, if at all. Steer clear of complex issues such as sour working relationships, mistreatment by a former or current company, position downgrades, or long-term unemployment.

- **Shows off your excellent communication skills**   The cover letter gives you a chance to "wow" the reader with your written communication skills. Trust me—most employment managers have seen their share of poorly written cover letters. Your well-thought-out and carefully written letter will be a breath of fresh air—and will help you land the interview!

Excellent communication skills are always an important plus in any career, from secretaries to truck drivers to management executives. Don't overlook the persuasive power of these skills!

- **Conveys your knowledge of the company**   The cover letter lets you show off your knowledge of company dynamics and your understanding of current industry needs. A little research goes a long way to impress even the savviest hiring manager.

- **Specifies your job objective as it relates to the job or company**
  Always write a cover letter that is tailored to a specific job or company. By doing so you can target your job objective to the current needs of the company. Your cover letter job objective may be a step or two more focused than your resume's more generic version.

 Be sure your job objective is reflected throughout the body of your letter. Keep the focus on your skills *as they relate to the job at hand.*

- **Presents you as a professional**   A crisp, professionally presented cover letter adds weight to the credentials on your resume.

 Filter out the fluff stuff! Once you've written your cover letter, edit it with an eye for brevity.

HOW YOUR COVER LETTER IS SCREENED

You may assume, like many other job seekers, that most cover letters receive only a passing glance from any hiring manager. Why, you ask, should I slave over a great cover letter when no one may even read it?

The truth is, cover letters are gaining in importance, and are more likely to be read now than ever before. This is because many hiring managers realize that resumes today are often written with significant help—either by a resume-writing service, an employment firm, or even by computer program. These outside services help to create error-free resumes, but they also eliminate many of the clues that employers look for when evaluating job candidates. More and more, hiring managers turn to the cover letter as the source of revealing and accurate information about a job candidate.

Employers like to screen cover letters for clues to a candidate's skills and attributes, particularly those that may not directly relate to the technical skills needed for the job. The following are some of the key elements being reviewed in your cover letter:

- **Spelling**   Many employers cringe at spelling errors in cover letters, and in some industries a spelling error means a one-way ticket to the trash. Spelling errors reveal a careless attitude and lack of attention to detail. Use a three-step editing process: First, use your computer's spell-check program to tackle any outright errors in your letter. Then, give it the eyeball test yourself. Third, have a friend (or friends) proofread it for you. Between these three steps, no spelling error should sneak through.

- **Grammar**   Poor grammar often means an immediate trip to the discard pile for your cover letter, and it takes your resume along with it. Shoddy grammar reveals poor communication skills, which are a high priority in almost any hiring situation. For a quick brush-up on grammar and letter-writing techniques, see chapter 11.

- **Format**   Your cover letter must make the right first impression with a traditional, neatly aligned format and a careful presentation. Inappropriate stationery, typos, smudges, or other sloppiness can put the kibosh on an otherwise excellent letter. Chapter 10 will give you the details on format.

- **Choice of content**   The toughest part of a cover letter is knowing what to say and how to say it. Culling just the right material from your extensive history and presenting it in a way that makes it impressive is not an easy task. Employers appreciate a concise letter that sticks to the point in a logical, easy-to-read framework.

- **Your skills**   Don't forget the point of the cover letter: to capture the attention and imagination of the reader so that he or she will want to learn more by reading your resume. The reader wants to know how your skills relate to the job opening at hand. Don't expect the reader to recognize all of your qualifications from reading your resume. Identify the skills needed for the available position and highlight them in your cover letter, using examples of past achievements to demonstrate your strengths. Put yourself in the place of the hiring manager and write the letter from that perspective.

- **Your personality**   Much more than the resume with its standardized format, the cover letter offers insight into your personality. The overall tone of the letter can project attributes such as confidence, creativity, or a positive attitude. By the same token, if you're bitter, indifferent, or desperate, you may leave clues in your writing that the reader will notice.

WHAT COVER LETTERS SHOULDN'T DO

A poorly written cover letter can do irreversible harm to your resume presentation. Remember, the cover letter creates that all-important first impression in the mind of the reader. If the reader is turned off by your letter, he or she may never move on to read your resume at all.

As you write your letter, avoid these deadly—yet common—errors:

1. **Do not BORE** Rambling, redundant, long-winded accounts of irrelevant skills do nothing to strengthen your resume. Neither do lengthy paragraphs and big chunks of text without a break. Be concise and stick to the point!

2. **Do not BEG** There is a fine line between a dignified request for consideration for a job and groveling. Be respectful, but not meek.

3. **Do not BRAG** Another fine line you need to walk is between a considered presentation of your related job skills, and a pompous pontification. You want to impress your reader with your accomplishments and skills without being overassertive or egotistical.

4. **Do not BLEED** The last thing a hiring manager wants to hear about is how you need this job to help pay the mortgage or because you have two kids in college this year. Including personal financial details in a cover letter is a definite no-no. So is any other sob story that is meant to make the hiring manager consider you for the job based upon your needs. Focus on the hiring manager's needs, not your own, when writing your letter!

CHAPTER SUMMARY

In this lesson, you learned the reasons why cover letters are imperative in today's job market, and why they are gaining popularity with hiring managers. You also learned how a well-written cover letter can empower your job search campaign.

CHAPTER 2

The Making of a Great Cover Letter

In this chapter, you will learn what separates a great cover letter from a poor one. You will also pick up some tips to make your cover letter shine above the rest, and see how to leave out information that can harm your job hunt.

AVOID THE "ORDINARY" COVER LETTER

Most job seekers think of a cover letter as nothing more than a polite introduction of the resume to the potential employer. They feel that the cover letter has no purpose other than to transmit the main document, the resume, to the hiring manager. With this in mind they write typical, unimaginative cover letters that look something like this:

August 23, 2000

Dear Mr. Clark,

I am interested in acquiring a position within your organization. Attached is a copy of my resume outlining my business experience, educational background, training, and skills. Please note my extensive background in administration, including four years as an Office Coordinator with Shel-Flor, Inc., a mid-size manufacturing firm. I would appreciate consideration for an administrative position in your company. I look forward to hearing from you.

Sincerely,

Janet Jobless

Janet Jobless

Writing this kind of bland transmittal letter can be a costly mistake. Don't miss the opportunity to direct the reader's attention to your strong points and job objective in a way that the resume can't.

ELEVEN TIPS FOR A GREAT COVER LETTER

As you'll read later in this book, there are particular cover letter strategies you should use to handle different situations in the job market. The letter you send to a company in response to an advertised job vacancy, for example, should differ from a letter you send "cold." To take care of all your job search needs, you may end up with three or four basic cover letter templates you can work from, editing and pasting to get it just right for each company you send it to.

Despite the differences in your letters, there are certain strategies that are important to employ no matter what kind of cover letter you are writing. The following tips are the things that turn good cover letters into *great* cover letters. Some will be discussed in more detail in the following chapters, but pay attention to each one here and remember them as you write your cover letter.

1. **Brief is best!** Keep your cover letter to one page only, except in very special circumstances. A great cover letter makes the most of the opportunity to sell your skills to the employer without taxing him or her with too much detail.

2. **Do your research.** Whenever possible, mention an article or other piece of information that will grab the reader's interest from the get-go. Referring to an article in the local paper or a tidbit from the company Web site will go a long way toward demonstrating that you are paying attention and know what is currently important in their world.

3. **Steer clear of generic formula letters.** Your letter shouldn't look like the same one you sent to 20 other companies, with the name and date changed at the top. Employers can spot a formula letter from miles away, and won't bother reading it because they know it can't have anything pertinent to say. Do your research to make your letter address the particular needs of the company! See chapter 14 on researching companies.

4. **Match your skills to their needs.** If you've done your research on the company, you have some idea what their business is about and how it might be changing or growing. Before you write your cover letter, be sure to discern what you think are the strongest needs of the

company, or the most desired skills for a particular position. Then focus your letter on the skills that you have that relate to those needs directly.

Be sure to complete the exercise in chapter 4 to determine your strongest skills. The exercise will guide you to your skills base and help you recognize the accomplishments you've achieved by putting these skills to use. You can then refer to these proven accomplishments in your cover letters to demonstrate your value in relation to the potential employer's needs.

Nobody wants to hire a rocket scientist if they aren't building rockets. Show them that you have *what they want.*

5. **No gimmicks!**   Some job seekers feel that the only way they can stand out from the crowd is to do something outrageously different in their cover letter and resume. While this strategy might impress managers in some of the highly creative fields such as graphics design or advertising, it simply falls flat in most business settings. Why? Because wildly unusual tactics don't follow the implied rules of professional business correspondence, and tend to make you look eccentric. Since the recipients of these cover letters don't know anything else about you, their first impression is only that you are "strange," desperate for a job, or just plain unprofessional.

6. **Address it to a person.**   A cover letter that is addressed "To Whom it May Concern:" doesn't start out on a very flattering note. Such a salutation is stiff, lifeless, and reveals a lack of knowledge of the organization you wish to work for. Make it mandatory that you find the name of the person to whom you are writing.

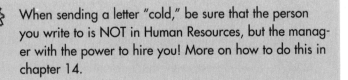

When sending a letter "cold," be sure that the person you write to is NOT in Human Resources, but the manager with the power to hire you! More on how to do this in chapter 14.

7. **Flaunt your accomplishments.** One of the most important rules you must follow as a job seeker is to prove what you can do by demonstrating what you've done. The best proof a potential employer has that you can produce results for him or her is to see that you've produced results for someone else.

> Give the reader specifics! Vague referrals to "superior results" or "excellent skills" tend not to ring true, and can portray you as boastful or unsure of your direction. Accomplishments and skills that have been specifically spelled out and quantified are the most impressive.

8. **Use a third-party endorsement.** A reference to a positive comment, performance review, or other recognition of your work is a convincing plus for any cover letter. If possible, include a compliment you've received such as, "Management described my latest project as *remarkably well-coordinated. Every element was brought to completion under budget and ahead of schedule.*" The remarks you refer to don't have to be officially written anywhere; a casual compliment is equally valid. Just be sure that your reference to these comments can be backed up if questioned.

9. **Mention someone the reader may know.** This tactic holds one of the strongest guarantees that your letter will get read. A letter that begins, "Our mutual friend, Mary Jo Johnson, suggested I get in touch with you" is almost always going to be given special consideration.

10. **Keep the tone positive and upbeat.** Don't go anywhere near anything negative! Don't mention a company layoff, a bad boss, a lack of advancement potential, etc. While these kinds of things may be completely beyond your control and have absolutely no reflection on your ability to do good work, they carry with them negative connotations. Here's the rule if you think something could in any way be construed as negative: When in doubt, leave it out!

Don't be defensive in your cover letter. Attempting to clear the air up front about getting fired or having bad chemistry with your co-workers will work against you every time. Save any explanations you may need to make for the job interview.

11. **Write it neatly.** Use 8½" × 11" paper that matches the resume bond and color. Type and print it to make an attractive, professional presentation. More on presentation and format in chapter 10.

FOUR COMMON MISCONCEPTIONS ABOUT COVER LETTERS

Many job seekers have mistaken impressions about how to write cover letters and use them effectively. Following are some of the most common misconceptions:

1. **Job seekers no longer need to send cover letters.** Many job seekers tell me they think the cover letter concept is outdated, and that employers no longer expect to receive them. I suspect that this erroneous rumor spread along with stories that many cover letters get tossed into the round file before getting so much as a glance.

   While it is true that some cover letters don't get read, it's usually because of poor packaging and bad initial impressions. I think it's safe to say that the vast majority of employers not only expect to see a cover letter with a resume, but consider an application package incomplete without one.

2. **Cover letters can be standardized forms with different names plugged in.** With the advent of word processors, many job seekers took advantage of the new technology to write one standardized cover letter template, and merely plugged in different company names at the top. This is a very handy idea indeed, but not one that is likely to win over an employment manager.

   People who hire see a lot of cover letters, and they can spot a standardized letter from the first sentence. Make yours specific to the job and particular to the company, and you'll win bonus points before your resume's even read.

3. **A cover letter shouldn't restate what is in the resume.** While it is true that you don't want to offer exactly the same information verbatim as it appears on your resume, it is perfectly acceptable to highlight the information that you want the reader to pay special attention to. Borrow some of the facts from your resume, but add more details to make your cover letter compelling.

4. **Electronic and faxed resumes don't need cover letters.** Remember this rule: Any time you send a resume, it should be accompanied by a cover letter. Faxed and e-mailed cover letters are no exception. Period.

SIX THINGS TO LEAVE OUT OF YOUR COVER LETTER

Cover letters are not long documents, so the little space you are given to write on is precious. Each word must count toward your overall purpose: to convince the reader that you are a viable job candidate worthy of an interview.

Too many cover letter writers waste this precious space by including things that are either unnecessary or even harmful to their purpose. Before you begin writing your letter, commit these rules to memory. Leave out of your cover letter:

1. **An open job objective**   Some cover letter writers figure that if they leave their job objective open or vague, they will put themselves in line for a wider variety of jobs, and be considered for a broader range of opportunities at the company. Unfortunately, a cover letter with a vague job objective will more likely remove you from consideration for most or maybe all jobs, because the reader can't get a feel for where you might fit in.

   Don't count on the reader to make the connection between your background and the company's job openings. You have to tell the reader what you want, so that you will be considered for the jobs that fit your skills and needs.

A specified job objective focuses the reader's attention on your strongest credentials, and suggests to the employer that you are organized and goal-oriented.

2. **Explanation of unemployment** There is no good reason for explaining in your cover letter why you are leaving your current employer. Yet many cover letter writers, especially those who have been separated from a company due to a massive layoff program, feel that an explanation is in order, to prevent the reader from suspecting poor job performance and its consequences.

These feelings may stem from the writer's concern that hiring managers view unemployment as a sign of a problem. Not so long ago, when companies kept employees in their ranks throughout their careers, and employees felt fierce loyalty to that company, unemployment was indicative of an employee who somehow couldn't tow the line. Hiring managers grew concerned when a job applicant was not cozily cocooned in a steady job.

Today, however, the term "steady job" is outmoded. Today's corporate environment no longer upholds the "company man" mentality, and most employees change jobs and companies quite often in the course of their career. Because of this job maneuvering, brief periods of unemployment are commonplace. In fact, the person reading your cover letter has probably experienced his or her own period of unemployment! Therefore, unemployment no longer carries the negative connotations of the past, and is unnecessary to defend in the cover letter.

3. **Salary history or expectations** Defining your specific salary parameters in the cover letter can only work against you. If, for example, you state in the cover letter that you wish to make $50,000 in your new position, and the company to which you sent the letter is willing to pay $48,000, you just knocked yourself out of the running for the job over a mere $2,000. Or, if the company was willing to pay $60,000, and you state in your letter that you wish to make $50,000, what do you think they are going to offer you? If they think you'll be happy with $50,000, they won't offer you $60,000.

Either way, you can't win the salary game by revealing your past, current, or desired compensation figures on your cover letter. Let the salary issue wait until you get the job offer. When you know they want you; *that's* the time to talk money. See chapters 8 and 9 for ways to handle the salary issue effectively in various situations.

4. **Explanations of potential problems**   Don't use the cover letter to bring up potential negatives such as health problems, pregnancy, negative job experiences, unusual scheduling requests, etc. No matter what your reason for including this information, it just isn't a good idea to call attention to potential negatives before you present the reader with all of your positives. Once you've established that positive impression, the negatives won't look quite so ominous.

5. **Your date of availability**   Don't state that you are not available to come to work until X date on your cover letter. It sends the message that you want to do things *your* way, regardless of the company's needs. Sure, there may be legitimate reasons why you can't start a job until a certain date. The trick is not to bring it up until later in the process, usually not until you've received the job offer.

> When writing your cover letter, don't forget that the reader is in charge: The reader is the one with the power to give you the time of day or chuck you in the foul file. Don't get on his or her bad side by attempting to assume any power at this stage. You have none, and the reader knows it.

6. **Irrelevant references**   Avoid listing job titles or responsibilities that don't support your job objective. You want to write a letter that is clear, concise, and focused, which means that all extraneous information must be painstakingly extracted.

CHAPTER SUMMARY

In this chapter, you learned tricks for turning an *ordinary* cover letter into a *great* one. You also learned important things to leave out of your letter and common misconceptions that plague cover letter writers.

CHAPTER 3

Skills Employers Look for Most

No two hiring managers are exactly alike. This makes it tough to know how to write a cover letter that is pleasing to every hiring manager you send it to. One person's ideal job candidate is another person's instant rejection.

There are certain factors, however, that are commonly regarded as positive qualities no matter what the job or who is reading the cover letter. It's important to know what these qualities are, and how to write them into your letter.

EVALUATING JOB CANDIDATES

Hiring managers typically evaluate a job candidate along two broad dimensions:

- **Job expertise** A job candidates' level of knowledge, skills, industry-related experience, and technical expertise as it relates to the job at hand.

- **Personal skills**   A candidate's unique set of personal behaviors and values, which allow him or her to achieve success in the particular position to be filled.

Most people assume that hiring managers place the strongest emphasis on level of experience (job expertise) when evaluating candidates. In reality, however, it is the personal qualities that go *beyond* the experience level that separate the mediocre job candidates from the hot prospects.

These personal qualities are largely revealed in the cover letter. The resume, with its terse, telegraphic wording and focus on job skills, is much less indicative of personality characteristics. Thus, when hiring managers read cover letters, they are looking for personality traits that will work well in their office setting, corporate culture, and for the responsibilities of the position.

QUALITIES HIRING MANAGERS LOOK FOR WHEN READING COVER LETTERS

A Strong Work Ethic

Your cover letters should include a brief description of the accomplishments you have achieved *beyond* your everyday duties. This shows the reader that you not only know how to do your job, but you know how to do it *well*.

HOW TO WRITE IT IN YOUR COVER LETTER: Include a bulleted section in your cover letter that lists three or four recent, impressive accomplishments. Focus your letter on these rather than the daily tasks and duties of your job. Spend the better part of the space describing what you personally contributed to the position by highlighting your accomplishments, special assignments you worked on, projects you managed or assisted with, or outstanding awards you received. Some letter writers find it effective to narrow their accomplishments list to one particularly strong accomplishment and spend more time on how it was achieved and how its results have added to the company. This might be written as, "Last quarter my sales team won $6 million in new business. Let me tell you why I think we were so successful…"

Enthusiasm

A hiring manager wants to hire an employee who has enthusiasm and energy for the job.

HOW TO WRITE IT IN YOUR COVER LETTER: Use lively language that conveys a positive attitude. For example, instead of:

"In my current position, I answer phones, taking calls from customers on a 10-line phone system."

Write it this way:

"In my current position, I enjoy dealing deftly and courteously with customers on a busy 10-line phone system."

 Keep your cover letter from being dry and lifeless by infusing it with a fresh tone. Give them the idea that you love your job!

Written Communication Skills

A hiring manager will assess your cover letter according to your written presentation. Do you have the ability to state things in a logical fashion? Are you able to use words to their best advantage? How is your spelling? Is your letter grammatically correct?

HOW TO WRITE IT IN YOUR COVER LETTER: Don't begin writing without organizing your thoughts first. Gather the information you need before putting pen to paper, and write an outline of the important points. After your first draft, don't be afraid to review your letter critically and edit deliberately.

People Skills

While it is true that the phrase "people skills" has been overused and borders on trite, it is still a quality that hiring managers value highly. An employee without the ability to get along with co-workers or clients often causes more headaches than he or she is worth.

Conveying a friendly attitude scores big points with any employer who has a job to fill.

HOW TO WRITE IT IN YOUR COVER LETTER: Highlight accomplishments or job duties that center on dealing with people. Making oral presentations, leading meetings, negotiating contracts, acting as a liaison, and supervising staff all require an ability to interact with people. Remember to emphasize not only that you did these things, but that you did them well.

Honesty

No employer wants to hire someone who is conniving, irresponsible, or deceitful. A cover letter should make the reader feel that the writer has integrity.

HOW TO WRITE IT IN YOUR COVER LETTER: While it is always a nice touch to quantify accomplishments with percentages and statistics, it's not wise to embellish achievements by making up numbers or overstating your results. This is often quite transparent to a seasoned hiring manager. Rather than coming across as a high achiever, you make it plain that you are willing to toy with the truth.

 If you are unsure of exact figures or percentages when quantifying results, it is safe to use the word "approximately" to indicate that the numbers may not be precise.

Confidence

As a job seeker, you must walk a fine line between conveying pride in accomplishments and appearing to have an overinflated ego. You must reach the right balance of stating your achievements without the appearance of bragging.

HOW TO WRITE IT IN YOUR COVER LETTER: Avoid words that make high claims unless you back them up with proof. For example, don't say "superior" management skills without including detailed job experience and specific results that support your claim.

Organizational Skills

Readers can't help but notice your organizational presentation as they peruse what you've written. They will evaluate your organizational capabilities and be impressed with a cover letter that conveys orderliness and linear thinking.

HOW TO WRITE IT IN YOUR COVER LETTER: Make sure that your cover letter follows a logical presentation. Group information logically, and keep your bulleted section consistent. To give your letter harmonious lines and a pleasing appearance, avoid bulky paragraphs.

A Positive Personality

It is difficult to assess a person's personality from a cover letter alone. Cover letters are not designed to delve into personality traits, and after all of your work experience, education, and other features have been presented, there usually isn't much space left over to devote to personal characteristics. Remember, though, that the more you can reveal about *who you are* as well as *what you can do*, the more comfortable they will feel with how well you can work for *them.*

HOW TO WRITE IT IN YOUR COVER LETTER: Feel free to give the reader as many clues as you can about your positive personality traits. Use descriptive words like "creative," "motivated," and "energetic," and be sure to include accomplishments that prove you are what you say you are!

 Refer to your skills assessment in chapter 4 to help you choose accurate descriptive words.

Up-to-Date

Employers like to know that you are keeping current in your field and that you care enough about your skills to keep them from growing stale.

HOW TO WRITE IT IN YOUR COVER LETTER: If you haven't mentioned current training on your resume, be sure to include it in your cover letter. Demonstrate that you are diligent about keeping your skills up-to-date by naming a few of the company-sponsored courses, workshops, classes, and seminars you've taken in recent years. This is especially important for people in the ever-changing field of technology.

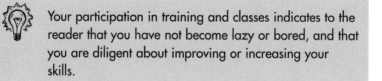

Your participation in training and classes indicates to the reader that you have not become lazy or bored, and that you are diligent about improving or increasing your skills.

CHAPTER SUMMARY

In this lesson you learned nine major qualities hiring managers look for when evaluating resumes, and how to write those qualities into your cover letter.

CHAPTER 4

Evaluate Your Skills

*In this chapter, you will complete an assess-
ment worksheet to help you identify your most
significant accomplishments and to determine
what skills you used in achieving them. This
enables you to write a cover letter that reflects
your strengths and achievements.*

WHY ASSESS MY SKILLS?

Skillful job hunters know who they are and what they have to offer, and
even their cover letters reflect this strong goal orientation and confidence.
Remember that a cover letter, like the resume, is a sales presentation, and
the product you are selling is you. It would be unwise to attempt to write
your sales brochure without having first developed a thorough knowledge
of your product.

As discussed in chapter 2, employment managers review cover letters with
an eye toward proven results. Hiring a new employee involves a great deal
of risk, but evidence of past successes shown through quantified achievements eases some of the hiring anxiety. Achievements prove not only that
you have the skills the hiring manager is looking for, but that you have the
qualities it takes to use those skills to achieve positive results.

In order to write a cover letter that highlights your successes as they relate to
the company or job at hand, you must do some preparation before writing the

actual letter. First, you must study the accomplishments and successes you have achieved through your life and career. If you have recently written your resume, you may have already identified key professional accomplishments and highlighted them on your resume. If you have not yet completed your resume, or if you're looking to boost your list of skills and accomplishments, complete the inventory exercise at the end of this chapter.

UNDERSTANDING ACCOMPLISHMENTS

An accomplishment is something that:

- You did well.
- You enjoyed doing.
- Involved a problem that you solved.
- You are proud of.

Accomplishments begin with situations or problems that call for action. You have taken steps to alleviate the problems, thereby achieving results.

An accomplishment does not have to relate to your school or work experience. It can be anything from your personal background as well. Some examples are:

- You planned a trip and traveled to Europe solo.
- You coordinated a conference for 180 people.
- You directed the annual PTA fund-raiser.

These are specific projects you took on at work, school, home, or in the community, and they all resulted in a quantifiable achievement.

 Don't overlook the results portion of your accomplishments. Employers will key in on results, especially if you can quantify them rather than make generalizations. Use words and numbers such as 25 percent savings, 15,000 unit increase, $65,000 each year, 12 direct report employees, etc.

UNDERSTANDING SKILLS

Each of your accomplishments can be broken down into a set of skills that you used to complete the task. For example, you can't compose a good poem without having good writing skills, and you can't direct a successful workshop without having good leadership skills. Don't just list your accomplishments—point out the skills you used in your achievement.

Don't be shy! Employers want to know if you have the skills to accomplish a particular job for them. Integrate some of your key accomplishments into the cover letter so employers will discern the skills that you have and assess whether you can put those same skills to use for them.

The Two Types of Skills

Employers attempt to evaluate two types of skills during the assessment process: learned skills and intuitive skills.

Learned Skills

Learned skills are those skills that you have been taught or that you have taught yourself somewhere along the way. They might be related to your current career, past positions, or other aspects of your life.

Examples of learned skills are:

- Rebuilding a car engine
- Driving a bus
- Planting a garden
- Running a computer program
- Hanging drywall
- Sewing a dress
- Managing a product line

Cooking a gourmet dinner is just as much a skill as launching a satellite; both involve learning new behaviors and gaining knowledge about the way things work and the steps involved in making certain things happen. In none of the cases above could a person know how to do these things without first learning how. A potential employer will be most interested in the learned skills that are closely related to the position for which you are applying.

Intuitive Skills

Intuitive skills, on the other hand, are those skills that you possess innately; they are part of your personality, and you can use these skills in many different situations.

Examples of intuitive skills are:

- Persistence
- Tidiness
- Efficiency
- Creativity
- Tenacity
- Honesty
- Precision
- Adaptability
- Punctuality

These are personality traits that you carry with you throughout life. As you can see, they are less specific than the learned skills, but they are no less important. These skills are transferable from one situation to the next: If you are honest in one situation, you are likely to be honest in another. Punctual people can be counted on to arrive on time, no matter what the setting or situation.

 Know your intuitive skills! Potential employers often pay more attention to intuitive skills than they do learned skills. Your intuitive skills, when backed with examples of accomplishments that prove their strength, will help set you apart from other job candidates.

THE FOUR-STEP SKILLS ASSESSMENT EXERCISE

Identifying your own skills and strengths is not difficult. Follow through the four steps of this simple exercise to compile your personal skills list.

1. List Your Six Favorite Accomplishments

These can be from any time in your life and can be as detailed or as simple as you want. You might include accomplishments from a childhood scouting project, the time you stood up to the bully on the playground, or the million-dollar account you landed last July.

Example:

> When I was 22 and had just graduated from college, I talked a group of my friends into spending six months with me on a backpacking trip of Europe. We had no money, no contacts, and very little knowledge, but we went anyway and had a ball.

2. Examine Why This Accomplishment Makes You Satisfied or Proud

Write your thoughts below each accomplishment.

Example:

1. I was able to convince my friends to spend a great amount of effort and time on a project I had conceived.

2. I had to do extensive research, planning, and coordinating just to get things off the ground.

3. It was a courageous thing to do.

4. I managed to get along in many different countries that had customs and language different from those of the U.S.

5. We survived for six months on practically no money. I came up with a few ingenious ways to save cash.

6. The five of us got along great for the entire six months despite close quarters, differing agendas, and dissimilar personalities.

7. It was a long-term project that I stuck with, despite a lack of support and other problems.

8. I learned to deal with foreign currency and various rates of exchange.

3. Filter Out the Skills

Examine each numbered statement above to discern the skills involved. Include even those skills that seem obvious or simple. List the skills on a separate sheet of paper.

> Don't overlook your basic skills. Many people who are assessing their skills overlook the most basic ones because they figure everyone has them and they are not worth listing. Remember that not everyone can do what you can do. Take care to include all skills.

Example:

1. *Convinced my friends*   Persuasion, tenacity, salesmanship, motivation, enthusiasm, and ability to motivate others

2. *Planned details of the trip*   Ability to conduct research, plan, coordinate, and arrange; organizational skills

3. *Did it even though I was a little bit afraid*   Courage, risk-taking, boldness, and self-confidence

4. *Adjusted to new customs*   Adaptability, flexibility, and ability to learn

5. *Survived six months on a tiny budget*   Ability to manage a budget, economical, and conservative

6. *Maintained friendships*   Ability to compromise, respectful of friendships, outgoing, and get along well with others

7. *Stuck with long-term project*   Determination, focus, drive, tenacity, vision, persistence, and self-confidence

8. *Learned foreign currency*   Attention to detail and knowledge of exchange rates

The backpacking trip accomplishment easily involves well over 30 deep-seated intuitive skills that are vital to success in any professional position. Hiring managers will be looking for these types of skills. In completing this exercise, you are preparing yourself with a list of your skills ready for the asking. Moreover, you have in hand more than a list of words—you have organized the proof (the accomplishments themselves) to back up the words!

4. Identify Your Most Predominant Skills

As you complete this exercise, some skills reappear under almost every accomplishment. These skills are a strong part of your personal skills set. Write the 10 most frequently occurring technical skills and the 10 most frequent intuitive skills below:

10 Technical Skills

10 Intuitive Skills

_____

_____

_____

_____

_____

_____

_____

_____

_____

CHAPTER SUMMARY

In this lesson, you learned to identify your unique accomplishments and skills using the four-step skills assessment exercise. You also learned why your skills and accomplishments are important to include on your cover letter.

CHAPTER 5

Traditional Cover Letters: Greetings and Opening Paragraphs

In this chapter, you will learn how and when to use a traditional cover letter, and examine samples of acceptable greeting and opening paragraphs.

THE TRADITIONAL COVER LETTER DEFINED

Traditional cover letters are the most common type of letter received by hiring managers. They are generally two to three brief paragraphs in length, and offer a synopsis of your skills and accomplishments in standard letter form. The traditional format is the one to use when targeting companies with no known job openings (when you're sending letters "cold").

The traditional cover letter should be used when you are addressing a company directly (rather than going though a recruiting firm), yet you have no information regarding the details of a particular job opening. In fact, you need not have heard of any particular job opening to send a traditional cover letter and a resume. All you need is the desire to work for that company.

This chapter will introduce you to a well-written traditional letter and walk you step-by-step through its first few sections. Chapters 6 and 7 will introduce the main body and the closing, respectively.

A SAMPLE "TRADITIONAL"

A hiring manager might receive hundreds of cover letters and resumes every month. A well-written traditional cover letter, one that stands out from the crowd of others, looks something like this:

April 10, 2000

Mr. Kurt Smith
Senior Development Specialist
XYZ Incorporated
One North Hill Plaza
Columbia, MD 21044

Dear Mr. Smith,

I have been following your development projects in several recent issues of the *Columbia Times*, and have been particularly intrigued by your multi-use facility project that is in the planning stages for Kendallville Park.

As an enthusiastic planner with degrees in Urban Planning and Environmental Design, please accept my application for employment with XYZ Incorporated. In following your recent development projects, I'm convinced that XYZ's background and planning needs match my skills directly.

I have had extensive experience in both economic development and in county planning. My economic development experience was as a Community Development Planner with Region 4B Development in Carson City, NV. My background includes:

- grant writing
- grant administration
- park planning
- small town planning
- ordinance writing

In the 17 months I was employed by Region 4B I wrote and received five different grants, which included a five hundred thousand dollar Community Development Block Grant (CDBG) for the town of Bakersville.

I am interested in relocating to the Columbia area and am very interested in joining your progressive and reputable firm. I will call you early next week to explore a time that we might meet to discuss potential opportunities at XYZ. I look forward to talking with you then.

Sincerely,

Sean Garrick

As you can see in the previous example, the traditional cover letter follows a standard business letter format with a formal heading and close, and two or three paragraphs of information. While there is no one perfect cover letter style, there are certain rules that most cover letters should follow. The previous letter effectively puts a few of those rules to use:

What the Letter Does Right

- The letter has a good length. Not too short, not too long. Just right.
- It begins with a catchy attention-getter. Nothing beats a little research.
- The letter writer states his or her purpose (looking for a job) early in the letter.
- It offers insight into his or her job search situation by mentioning interest in relocating to the area.
- The writer mentions that his or her skills match the company's needs.
- The letter gives specific examples, in bullet form, of particular skills that would be of interest to the company.
- The writer cites one specific example of an accomplishment that saved his or her previous employer money (or time).
- The letter takes a proactive stance with the follow-up in the close. The writer does not wait for the potential employer to call him.

THE ADDRESS

Traditional cover letters are written in a standard business format. The page should begin with the day's date, then the full name (including middle initial, if known), title, and address of the letter's intended reader, such as:

October 29, 2000 (today's date)

Ms. Janet Evans (recipient's name)
V.P. Operations (title)
Tri-State Data (company name)
15 Twin Knoll South (street address)
Heritage, OH 45077 (city, state, zip)

Dear Ms. Evans,

I have recently . . . (the letter continues from there)

Some letters include the sender's return address as well. This is a more formal style of business letter, and is set up like this:

Lorraine Taylor
7575 Yammasee Ct.
Clifton, MS 79809

October 29, 2000

Howard G. Sheltraw, MD
Director of Health Services
Liberty Medical Plaza
432 Amsterdam Blvd.
Albany, NY 29080

Dear Dr. Sheltraw,

I noticed in the September issue of . . . (the letter continues
from there)

 Notice that the addresses contain the business title of the recipient. These convey respect for the person to whom you are writing, and ensure that your letter gets to the right place in case of a recent personnel change.

In some cases, it may be best to add the department or function in which the person is employed, unless it is already included in the person's job title, as follows:

Mr. Joel P. Chase, Director
Public Affairs Department
Gannering and Finch, Inc.
Five Bunting Blvd.
Morgantown, WV 57903

Following standard business letter protocol, street numbers are normally spelled out up to ten; over ten may be written in numeral form.

Notice how abbreviations should be handled in business correspondence:

- The words "Street" and "Avenue" are not typically abbreviated, but "Boulevard" is typically abbreviated as "Blvd."
- Post Office Box is written "P.O. Box."
- You may abbreviate state names.
- It is acceptable to use abbreviations such as "Co.," "Corp.," or "Inc." within a company name, but follow the standard practice for the particular business you are addressing.

THE NAME

What's in a name? When it comes to a cover letter, just about everything. Using the correct name is pivotal in getting the response you are looking for from your targeted company.

I've seen thousands of cover letters that begin with that old stand-by, "To Whom It May Concern." I've seen perhaps thousands more that begin with "Dear Sir or Madam" or "Dear Employer." Unfortunately, these types of salutations say one thing loud and clear:

- You didn't do any research on the company.
- You know absolutely nothing about the company.
- You didn't care enough about the company to find out anything more.

Put yourself in the hiring manager's shoes. If you were hiring for a position and you received two identical letters, one addressed to "To Whom It May Concern" and the other addressed with your real name and title, which letter would you respond to more positively? Obviously, using the correct name for the person to whom you are sending the letter can have a tremendous impact.

Finding the Names

Many traditional cover letters are sent "cold," with no knowledge of any job opening, and no inside contacts to help you along the way. So how do you find the name of the person to whom you'd write the letter? In "cold" cases, this can require a bit of research, but the benefits of addressing your letter to a specific person far outweigh the time cost it takes to find the name.

Try these tips for finding names of managers:

- Call the receptionist and ask! OK, I admit, this one sounds like a pretty obvious thing to do. Yet why is it that so few job seekers are willing to pick up the phone and make the call? It isn't difficult or risky. Simply tell the receptionist that you have a letter to send to the department manager, and ask for the name and how to spell it!

  Make sure that you clarify all the details while you have the receptionist on the phone. If the manager's name is not gender specific, ask whether you should use "Ms." or "Mr." Also, ask for the manager's exact job title, so that you're sure to address your letter correctly.

> Don't tell the receptionist what type of letter you intend to send. If you mention that you are a job seeker, she may reroute you to personnel, which is not where you want to go. If she asks the nature of your business, tell her something cryptic, such as, "A friend suggested I send him some business materials" or "I'm running an idea by her . . . she'll understand when she sees it."

- Try the company Web site. If you don't know the Web address, call the company and ask. You might find just the name you're looking for, plus other valuable information. Many Web sites list key personnel and some even have short bios that discuss each manager's education, work history, and experience.
- The library is filled with wonderful business reference books that are up-to-date and loaded with information about companies of all sizes. You'll find the names of department heads, as well as other tidbits about subsidiaries, acquisitions, and other company news.
- Ask friends and acquaintances if they know anyone who works at the company you're interested in. Chances are, someone knows someone with whom you can begin the networking process, thereby greatly increasing the odds that you will someday land a job there!

For details on conducting company research, see chapter 14.

ADDRESSING THE READER

Now that you've found the name, how do you begin the letter? Is it acceptable to use first names? How formal should one be?

For the safest and most traditional salutation format, follow these rules:

- The addressee's name should always be preceded by a courtesy title, such as "Mr." or "Ms." This connotes a measure of respect for your reader.

- Don't use first names in the salutation unless you have a friendship with the person to whom you are writing. Business correspondence should be professional and respectful. Leave the "Dear Susan" or "Dear Tom" for your personal letters.

- Don't use the formal name in its entirety. I've seen letters that open with "Dear Barbara T. Small" and "Dear Ronald J. Pettyman III." In these cases, the salutation line should read "Dear Ms. Small" and "Dear Mr. Pettyman."

- In the case of a professional title such as "Dr." or "Col.," use the professional title in your salutation, such as "Dear Dr. Dorning."

- When addressing a woman without a professional title, it's acceptable to use the salutation "Ms." for both married and single women, such as "Dear Ms. Strohmeyer."

THE OPENING PARAGRAPH

The opening paragraph is designed to capture the reader's attention and to compel the potential employer to want to meet you personally to learn more about your skills and potential.

Many traditional cover letters open with a very predictable and mundane phrase. In similar words they basically say, "Please accept my resume for review. I am interested in working for your company." Not exactly heart-stopping information. In fact, when your cover letter's first sentence is predictable, the reader is likely to assume that the rest of the letter will be predictable too, and therefore not worth reading. This opening is not likely to capture the attention of a hiring manager or sway the opinion of a potential employer in a positive direction.

You must seize the reader's attention immediately by saying something interesting, and proving that this letter is not one of those mass-mailed generic types that aren't worth his time. How do you do this? Three attention-getters stand out as especially successful: the referral, the inside scoop, and the compliment.

The Referral

If you want to catch your reader's attention, tell her right away that you have a connection with someone she may know. Your connection doesn't have to be a high-ranking member of the company boardroom. It doesn't even have to be someone whose name the reader will immediately recognize. Of course, if your referral does have impressive credentials, all the better. But using any name will compel the reader to continue on with your letter, and gives you a chance to shine as you offer a sample of your background and accomplishments.

Using a name helps you in these ways:

* The reader probably assumes that the person you mentioned would recommend your skills to the company.

* When you come with a recommendation, the employer feels more confident about the validity of your skills and background. The more an employer trusts in you, the more comfortable he feels about the risk of hiring you.

* Using a name makes the reader feel that she has a connection to you already, which separates you from the massive stacks of anonymous wannabes.

Whenever possible, let your contact know that you plan to use his or her name in your cover letter. This reduces the risk of negative surprises for everyone concerned and demonstrates to the hiring manager that you know how to cover your bases.

Try these referral statements on for size:

- "Debbie O'Strowski, in your Bethesda office, suggested that I contact you and let you know about my extensive background in brand management."
- "Because of my expertise and your current company expansion into the consumer housewares market, Bob Worley mentioned that you might have an interest in talking with me."
- "I was speaking with Sandy Arulf yesterday, and she mentioned that your company is a great place for a hardworking loan officer like me to put my skills to work."
- "Our mutual friend and colleague Ellen Dillon felt that my seven years in early childhood education might be of interest to you."
- "An employee of yours, Carl Morgenstern, has told me enthusiastically that XYZ Incorporated is not only a leader in the local advertising arena, but is a great place for an energetic graphic artist like me to put my creative talents to work."
- "Perry Odieson, your Director of Total Quality, told me about the statistical work that you are planning in pharmaceutical research. As a Senior Statistician with PharmaTech, this is a subject with which I am very familiar."

As you can see from these examples, each paragraph begins with a specific name mentioned in the very first sentence.

> If you don't know anyone in the organization in which you would like to work, try networking through a professional association. Or call the chamber of commerce and ask for an industry association roster. You may find key contacts whom you can call and engage in conversation about the company.

The Inside Scoop

Another effective attention-grabber is to show off your knowledge of the company by talking about current issues, trends, or recent changes within the organization or industry. This impresses the reader in several ways:

- It tells the reader that you care enough about working for the company that you took the time to learn about them.

- It convinces the reader that you are knowledgeable in your industry and your chosen field.

- It proves to the reader that you know how to conduct research and approach a task (in this case, writing a cover letter) with diligence.

Here are some effective "company knowledge" paragraphs:

- "I recently read an article in the *West Chester Pulse* concerning Celcorp's satellite offices expanding to the West Chester area. I will be graduating with a bachelor's degree in computer engineering in June, and would be very interested in joining a progressive and innovative firm like Celcorp."

- "Your company Web site states that in the past two years, Glenmore and Paris has taken a lead role in the manufacture of industrial application polyurethane foams. The fact that your sales have risen from 4.7 million to over 30 million in such a short time proves that you have innovative and effective leadership. I think my management style would blend well with G&P's proven leadership systems, and I would like to join your progressive team."

- "I read with interest the article in *Southern Iowa Business Journal* regarding your consumer electronics manufacturing facility in Bright, Iowa. The facility was rated as one of the highest-profit manufacturing plants in the southern Iowa region. In fact, Block and Boerger's profits have been soaring since the acquisition of the plant in 1997. My background in operations and my respect for your company make me a likely addition to your successful organization."

- "Your company name caught my attention in the Mutual Funds Report recently. My research indicates you have an exceptional record over the past three years, which shows outstanding portfolio management. I have five years' experience as a market analyst, and I believe I could make significant contributions to your proven organization."

- "TutorTime Learning Centers was cited in *The Academic* as being at the forefront of the emerging trend in tutorial learning services. I can imagine that the services you provide in your busy offices require extensive and careful administrative support. With my five years of administrative experience, I would excel in a fast-paced office like yours."

- "An article in the *Groveland Gazette* mentioned that you will be opening Groveland Hospital's new maternity wing on August 4. It sounds like you may be needing some additional hospital support staff! With seven years of experience in medical record-keeping, my background may be of interest to you at this time of growth for Groveland."

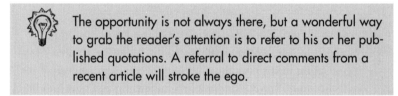

The opportunity is not always there, but a wonderful way to grab the reader's attention is to refer to his or her published quotations. A referral to direct comments from a recent article will stroke the ego.

The Compliment

Another way to ensure you've got the reader's attention is with a compliment. We all enjoy hearing or reading nice things about ourselves. Starting a cover letter on such a positive note makes the reader feel that much more positive about you. One word of warning, however: Your compliment must sound sincere. Outright flattery will get you nowhere.

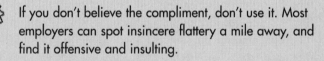

If you don't believe the compliment, don't use it. Most employers can spot insincere flattery a mile away, and find it offensive and insulting.

As you begin your letter, talk about a topic that interests your intended reader, and how his or her company, department, or even personal work has been noteworthy. Some examples:

- "In your tenure as economic administrator with Carroll County, you have made impressive headway in tackling the business district revitalization problems that have plagued the county for years. As a community planner, I have watched the significant progress you have made in this battle, and applaud your tenacity and vision.
- "Your department's aggressive advertising strategies have made CELLO Inc. one of the industry's top Widget manufacturers. As a

recent University of Pennsylvania graduate with a degree in advertising, I am impressed with your ability to make CELLO a household name."

- "Five years was all it took you to turn a small home-based services company into a local giant. In that short time, you have cornered the local insurance services market and are continuing your pattern of steady growth."

- "I have long admired Fenn-Kline's reputation as a strong and stable leader in the custom building products industry. Your pattern of steady growth in a market notorious for its wide fluctuations is extraordinary."

You are a professional, not a gushing groupie. Once you've printed the praise, move on, and move on quickly. Laying it on too thick can make you seem insincere or immature.

CHAPTER SUMMARY

In this chapter, you learned to address your cover letter, and open it with a hard-hitting first paragraph.

CHAPTER 6

The Traditional Cover Letter: The Main Body

In this chapter, you will learn the three sections you should include in the body of your cover letter, and how to write them to impress a hiring manager.

THE BODY

The body of the traditional cover letter must not lose the competitive edge you've established with your dynamic first paragraph. Your opening lines convinced the hiring manager to read on, and now you must make her glad she did.

The body of the cover letter is the place for you to describe your background and skills, and point out the value you can bring to the hiring organization. You have two to three paragraphs to let the reader know what you are all about, and how you can help with the needs of the company.

There are three important areas your cover letter should cover: purpose for writing, background summary, and skills and accomplishments.

YOUR PURPOSE FOR WRITING

Be very careful to let the reader know why you are writing to her, and exactly what type of position you're looking for. Even if you are not answering a newspaper ad and do not know what types of positions the company has available, you must have a stated job focus. This is not the place to be vague in hopes that you might leave yourself open for more job possibilities. In reality, a lack of clarity here often results in a trip to the "out" pile, since a reader with 20 cover letters in front of her doesn't have time to comb through your letter and connect all the dots.

Be specific in your job search focus. For example:

Don't say:

"I am interested in working for XYZ Corporation."

Instead, say:

"I am interested in a customer service position."

Don't say:

"I am interested in joining your sales department."

Instead, say:

"I am interested in a district sales manager position."

Don't say:

"I am interested in joining your marketing management team."

Instead, say:

"I am interested in a senior marketing management position."

The more specific you can be the better.

 Being specific doesn't mean making demands on the company. Don't specify things like hours, shift, or schedule. You can clarify these details once you get the job offer.

YOUR BACKGROUND SUMMARY

Include in the body of your cover letter a brief summary of your work history and education. The background summary usually includes the academic degree you've earned (including your major field of study), and offers a brief synopsis of relevant work experience.

Many letter writers argue that this same information can be found on the resume, and is therefore redundant in a cover letter. It is true, perhaps, that much of the information in the cover letter background summary is found in the resume. But the cover letter format allows you to give the information a different presentation; here, you can relate your experience directly to the needs of the letter reader. The cover letter permits to you to make a direct connection between your skills and the company's needs—something that the generic resume can't do.

> Many cover letter writers dangerously assume that the reader will be able to connect skills with needs simply by reading the resume. This is not always the case, especially if the reader is a generalist in human resources.

Remember, your cover letter must be captivating enough to stand on its own, regardless of how well written the resume is. If your cover letter doesn't capture the attention of the hiring manager, your resume may never even get a glance.

Five Rules for Your Background Summary

When writing your background summary, follow these rules:

- **Assume that the reader knows nothing about you or your field.**
  Offer specific details and descriptive phrases. Quantify whenever possible, and add definitive statements to create a clearer picture in the reader's mind. For example, don't say, "I worked in quality control for a medical technology company." Instead, say, "I was a quality control shift supervisor at the largest medical technology company in the mid-Atlantic."

• **Maintain a confident, upbeat style.** Attitude and chemistry go a long way in the hiring process, in the long run beating out even experience itself. Many cover letter writers may not realize it, but the reader will make determinations about your personality by sensing your attitude and behavior through the tone of your letter. So let your charisma shine through by choosing a lighter, less formal tone. Try not to use too much stilted, formal, bureaucrat-ese. This is not to say that you should become overly familiar, either. Simply write your letter in a style that reflects a confident, positive attitude.

• **Don't offer a dry listing of your duties and responsibilities.** Never use the phrase "I was responsible for . . . " or "My duties included . . . " on either your resume or your cover letter. Try to include your background summary in the context of your accomplishments, or as an intro to another thought.

Don't say:

> "As a staff Writer at American Life Insurance, my responsibilities included writing marketing brochures, editing a weekly newsletter, and developing promotional items."

Instead, say:

> "My three years as a staff writer at American Life Insurance taught me the importance of effective time management skills. As I balanced my usual tasks of editing the newsletter and creating promotional items, I was able to initiate and write a regular promotional advice column in the regional newspaper, which gave our company a strong, customer-friendly presence in the Delaware region."

• **Delete the detail.** Too much detail in your cover letter is a killer, because all that extra information detracts from the good stuff and wraps it up in so much "fat" that the reader may decide the few tasty morsels of information he might find hidden in there aren't worth the time. Away goes your letter, into the "ding" pile.

• **Be specific to their needs.** As you do your company research, keep an eye out for something to relate your skills to. Is the company growing in a certain area? Have they recently landed a new account? Are they working on a certain project you've read about? Consider these things as you compose your background summary, and tie your skills to the needs of the company.

Don't just say:

> "I have three years' experience at Horne and Doensch as an
> administrative specialist."

Connect their needs with your strengths, like this:

> "To facilitate the successful start-up of your new corporate
> offices, you are probably in need of administrative personnel with
> experience in a start-up corporate setting. I have three years' expe-
> rience in the newly opened offices of Horne and Doensch, where I
> learned the importance of strong organizational skills in a start-up
> situation."

Don't just say:

> "I have worked for six years as a sales associate at Tri-Arch,
> Incorporated."

Instead, give the reader a sense of how your skills can help his or her
company, with:

> "While my six years in sales at Tri-Arch would certainly apply to a
> sales management position with your firm, I think my familiarity
> with the bidding process and with blueprints would be an addi-
> tional and quite essential asset at American Architects."

YOUR SKILLS AND ACCOMPLISHMENTS

As an employer reads a cover letter, he is scanning for tangible evidence of
your skills and abilities that will add value to his organization.

Employers know that the best predictor of future performance is past performance in the same or similar areas.
Tell them what you've done—this proves what you *can*
do!

How do you convince a potential employer that you have the skills and abilities he is looking for? Use examples of past performance—in the form of specific accomplishments that you have achieved in your recent past. These can be from your work environment, a volunteer experience, a community event you helped to organize, and so on. Be careful to choose your accomplishments wisely or they could backfire and detract from your case.

In deciding what skills and accomplishments to highlight, pay careful attention to these key questions:

- **Does the skill or accomplishment match the needs of the organization for whom you wish to work?** If not, what good is it to highlight it? If you spend your entire letter focusing in on your independence and creativity when their main concern is hiring someone who can follow directions, you have just written yourself right out of a job offer.

- **Is the accomplishment or skill specific enough to make a definite impression?** Many letter writers fall into the negative tendency of watering down their specifics with words like "significant" and "major."

  For example, don't say:

  "Made significant improvements to accounts payable system." Since the word "significant" is a subjective term, the reader is unable to interpret whether your improvements were important to him or not.

  Instead, say:

  "Revamped accounts payable system to reduce paper processing time, saving the company the cost of overtime pay for three employees." This sentence makes the writer's accomplishment very clear.

- **Have you specified the result of your accomplishment?** A specific result packs more punch than a mere skill or accomplishment left hanging. This is a common mistake of cover letter writers, so be aware!

  For example, don't just say:

  "Designed, produced, and presented telephone skills workshop for new customer service employees."

Instead, say:

> "Designed, produced, and presented telephone skills workshop for new customer service employees, which improved customer satisfaction rate by 40 percent in first year."

 If you don't have specific numbers to plug into your cover letter, use words like "approximately," "in the range," or "saved an estimated" to help you quantify honestly.

- **Have you expanded upon the information in your resume?** If your cover letter does nothing but recite the very things you have included on your resume, why should anyone choose to read it? Your cover letter must provide new information to be worth its weight. It should take the generic information provided on your resume and connect it to the company you are writing to in a powerful and individualized way.

Make Your Accomplishments Section Shine!

Your accomplishments are an important part of your cover letter because they demonstrate what you can do for the potential employer. Here are four ways to make sure your accomplishments get the attention they deserve.

1. **Limit your list.** Choose only the top two to four accomplishments that relate directly to the job at hand. If you list more than four, the strength of each gets diluted.

2. **Use bullets.** Some writers prefer to draw attention to their accomplishments by bulleting them in the body of the letter. Bullets draw the eye, so using them gives your accomplishments added emphasis.

 If you have only one accomplishment that you wish to list in your letter, do not bullet it separately. Instead, include the accomplishment in the body of your text.

3. **Be direct.** Your accomplishments will pack more punch if they are powerful impact statements rather than several sentences full of details. One to two sentences should be all you need per accomplishment.

4. **Use examples.** The most powerful accomplishment statements are those that offer specific examples of problems solved and results achieved. Don't water things down with vague references.

CHAPTER SUMMARY

In this chapter, you learned the steps to take to keep the body of your cover letter concise, interesting, and informative.

CHAPTER 7

The Traditional Cover Letter: The Close

In this chapter, you will learn how to write an effective closing paragraph that advances the purpose of your cover letter and continues to sell the potential employer on your value and skills.

There are three important parts to a closing paragraph: the action statement, the "how I can be reached" statement, and the statement of appreciation.

THE ACTION STATEMENT

So far, your cover letter has been a well-honed sales presentation of your skills and background as they match the needs of your potential employer. But any Sales 101 professor would tell you that no presentation is complete without the assertive close—clinching the sale, so to speak. How do we move your letter from the "here is what I can offer you" stage to the next step forward?

You must close your letter with a statement of action, letting the potential employer know what your next move is. Tell the employer that you intend to take action by calling to determine interest and, if appropriate, arrange for a meeting or job interview.

Some examples of effective action statements are:

- "I will call you early next week to discuss the possibilities for me at AeroTech."
- "I will call you later this week to introduce myself and see if my resume is of interest to you."
- "I will call you mid-week to see if we might arrange a personal meeting."

Six Keys to an Effective Action Statement

When writing the action statement, it can be quite difficult to tread the thin line between confidence and cockiness. One false move can leave the reader with an unpleasant impression that taints your entire presentation.

As you write your action statement, consider these key factors to help you say what you want to say in just the right way:

1. **Be assertive, not aggressive.** Watch your language carefully so that you don't sound as if you are backing your reader into a corner. The idea is to sound tenacious and confident, yet respectful and polite. By the way, never assume you can show up at the office uninvited; the next step warrants a phone call, not a personal visit.

   NO: "I will drop by your office on Friday, February 11, for an informal visit."

   NO: "Please make yourself available for my call on Thursday, March 12, at 3:00."

   YES: "I will call you early next week to see if we might find a convenient time to meet."

2. **Give yourself some leeway on the time you are to follow up.** Don't put yourself in a difficult position by setting an impossibly narrow time frame in which to call your prospective employer. Letters that state, "I will call you on Wednesday, January 4 at 10:00" are hard to follow through with. They also appear arrogant by assuming that

the employer will be free then, or worse, implying that she should make herself free at the time you've dictated to await your all-important phone call. It is more appropriate to allow a two- to three-day window of calling time, such as, "I will call you early next week" or "I will follow up with you toward the end of the week."

NO: "I will call you on Wednesday, March 4, at 3:00."

NO: "I look forward to talking with you on Friday, January 3, between 2:30 and 3:00."

YES: "I will call your office early next week to follow up."

Be sure to allow yourself one or two days after you expect the letter to arrive on the employer's desk before you call. Thus, if you expect the letter to reach the employer's desk on Tuesday, you might mention that you'll call "later in the week." This doesn't preclude you from calling on Wednesday, and it gives you a chance to call back on Thursday or Friday if you don't reach him the first time. If you expect the letter to reach his desk on Friday, write that you'll call "early next week."

3. **Put the responsibility on your own shoulders.** Let the potential employer know that you will follow up with him, rather than waiting for him to follow up with you. It could be a long, boring wait by a silent telephone if you put the responsibility for the phone call on him. You have initiated the contact by letter—now it is your responsibility to further the contact through a telephone call.

NO: "I look forward to hearing from you regarding my resume in the near future."

NO: "If you find my resume interesting, please call me."

YES: "I will call you later this week to see if we might arrange a personal meeting."

4. **Don't be cocky.** Statements such as "I'll be expecting your call today!" or "Don't miss this opportunity to hire a quality candidate like me!" sound overconfident and immature. Such puffery doesn't

tend to sit well with hiring managers, so it's better to steer clear of overinflated statements like these.

NO: "To hire a top-level manager with outstanding skills, call me today!"

NO: "Considering my terrific qualifications, I will expect to hear from you in the near future."

YES: "I am confident that you will find my skills of interest, and will call you later in the week to see if we might arrange a time to meet face to face.

5. **Don't use wimpy language.**   On the other hand, you should be careful not to sound overly tentative or self-deprecating. Statements like "I hope to hear from you soon" or "I'll try to reach you next week" make you sound meek and unsure of yourself. Words like "hope" and "try" make you sound a bit like you're giving up before you even pick up the phone.

NO: "I'll leave a message with your receptionist if I can't reach you."

NO: "I know you are a busy person, but I would appreciate a call if you are at all interested in my resume."

YES: "I will call you on Monday or Tuesday of next week to discuss any opportunities at BenchMark."

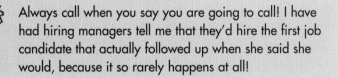

Always call when you say you are going to call! I have had hiring managers tell me that they'd hire the first job candidate that actually followed up when she said she would, because it so rarely happens at all!

6. **Don't plead.**   Some job seekers think that a strong close means a desperate attempt to get the letter reader's sympathy. Be careful not to sound like a hard-luck job seeker who has had his or her share of rejections. Watch out for closing statements such as "It is very important that I talk with you later this week. My current job ends in just two days" or "I sincerely hope that you will let me talk with you

when I call on Friday. If you'll just give me a chance, you'll like what I have to say."

NO: "I have so much more to tell you if you'll just take the time to listen."

NO: "Please don't pass up my resume. It has always been my dream to work at ABC."

YES: "I'll call you later in the week to see if we might schedule an interview."

THE "HOW I CAN BE REACHED" STATEMENT

This statement is perhaps the most basic and easily written portion of the cover letter. It has but one goal: to simply inform your reader how you can be reached. You may choose to include telephone numbers at home or at work, your e-mail address, or even a pager number if you are always on the go.

Here are a few examples of "how I can be reached" statements:

- "I can be reached at (522) 555-1212."
- "Should you wish to contact me, I can be reached at (522) 555-1212, or by e-mail @AOL.com."
- "You can contact me at home (522) 555-1212, or at the office (522) 555-7878."

There are just a few basic rules to follow:

- **Don't overdo it.**   Don't offer the reader a long list of every conceivable way you can be reached. Include only one or two communications options. Of course, you'll want to include the numbers at which you are most likely available. Your communications options may include pager, cell phone, home phone, work phone, and fax numbers, as well as e-mail address.

- **Consider confidentiality.**   If you want to keep your boss and co-workers from learning about your job search, you might be wise to leave your work phone and office e-mail address off of your cover letter. A home e-mail and phone number that you can check frequently puts you in control of incoming communication from potential employers.

- **Don't include dead-end numbers.** Be careful not to include negative numbers—those that lead to a potentially bad situation. These might include a hostile boss at your work number, a cell phone number that rings endlessly with no hope of being answered, or an e-mail address that only gets checked once every couple of weeks.

- **Make sure your home phone is primed and ready.** Make the kids aware that important phone calls may be coming in for you. Teenagers should be advised to pass along all messages to mom and dad. Younger children should be told not to answer the phone except in an emergency for the duration of your job search, to prevent your potential new boss from having an unexpected conversation about teddy bears with your four-year-old.

- **Record a professional-sounding message.** When you have sent cover letters and resumes to potential employers, there is always a possibility that they may call your home unexpectedly. Be prepared: You may want to change your whimsical answering machine message to one that sounds more professional. Keep it brief, and don't play music or permit any background noises. Try something like, "You have reached 555-1212. Please leave a message, and we'll return your call as soon as possible. Thank you." When your job search has ended successfully, you can go back to a less formal message if you prefer.

- **Don't offer a limited window of time when you are reachable.** The easier you make it for employers to reach you, the more likely it is that they will call you for an interview. Conversely, the narrower your "reachability window," the narrower your chances of landing a job. Thus, it is not wise to tell a potential employer "I can be reached on Monday evenings between 6:00 and 8:00" or "Because of my heavy schedule, I can only be reached by e-mail."

  Even such gentle phrases as "The best days to reach me are Mondays, Wednesdays, and Fridays" could cause employers to consider you hard to reach if their schedule conflicts with yours. Your best bet is to give a number that is not limited to time constraint, or you may find that busy hiring managers won't bother trying to fit their hectic schedule into your narrow time frame.

Invest in an answering machine and let it take calls for you if it is not a convenient time for you to carry on a professional conversation. If the dog is barking or the kids are screaming, let the machine take a message and call back at a quiet time when you are able to concentrate. Don't forget to check the messages regularly so you don't miss an important call.

THE STATEMENT OF APPRECIATION

A polite and courteous closing statement does much to warm the heart of a letter weary reader. Hiring managers tell me that when reading heavy stacks of cover letters, those that express appreciation for their time and interest stand out from the others. It doesn't take much time or space to add a little thank you at the end of your letter, and it can pay off in big dividends. Try these on for size:

"Thank you for your consideration."

"Thanks for taking the time to review my application."

"Thank you for your interest."

"I appreciate your time and consideration."

Easy enough!

PUTTING IT ALL TOGETHER

Now take a look at some full closing paragraphs, where all three pieces—the action statement, the "how I can be reached" statement, and the statement of appreciation—have been put together:

- "I will call you early next week to see if we might arrange an interview. If you would like to reach me in the meantime, you may call (513) 555-1212, or e-mail me at BGOODE@HOTMAIL.com. Thank you for your time and consideration."

- "I will call you by mid-week to introduce myself and see if we might arrange a personal meeting. Or, you can reach me at (414) 555-1212. Thank you for taking the time to review my qualifications."

- "I will be in touch with you early next week to discuss the possibilities at Smythe. If you would like to contact me, you may call me at (414) 555-1212, or e-mail me at HALFORD@EROLS.com. Thank you for your interest."

THE FINAL CLOSE

The Closing Line

The line at the end of your letter brings your message to a close. The appropriateness of the closing depends upon your relationship with the potential employer. Read the following sample closing lines.

Closing lines for formal, professional relationships:

Sincerely,

Sincerely Yours,

Yours Truly,

Very Truly Yours,

Closing lines for more informal professional acquaintances:

Yours,

Best Regards,

Best Wishes,

All the Best,

Note that each word in the closing line begins with a capital letter (except for "the").

 Take care to check your spelling! Many letter writers tend to misspell the words "Sincerely" and "Truly." You've nearly made it to the end of the letter—don't blow it now with a misspelled word.

Signature Line

Include a typed signature line at the end of your letter, placed flush with the closing line and about four lines below it. This leaves room for you to sign your name in pen in between.

The typical signature line includes the full formal name of the writer, with a first name, last name, and middle initial. If you feel that this seems overly formal for your cover letter, you may soften the tone of the signature line by signing more informally. Thus, the name "William K. Burke" might be signed "Bill Burke." The typed portion should remain "William K. Burke," however.

If you are sending your cover letter to a well-known business acquaintance, you may choose to sign your letter with your first name only.

The Name Game

Some letter writers face confusing issues when it comes to the signature. Follow these guidelines concerning your name on the cover letter:

- Match the signature line on your cover letter to your resume name. If you used a nickname on your resume, or wrote out your name with a full title, have the signature line on your cover letter match your name as it appears on your resume. This will avoid confusion and promote consistency.

- Always leave off formal titles Mr., Ms., and Mrs. in your signature line and signature.

- Beware of using the surname "Senior" on your cover letter. It hints at your age and reveals that you have a child.

- If your name does not identify your gender (such as Chris or Terry), you might be sure to write out your full name on the signature line, and sign the letter in the way that you prefer to be addressed. Thus, "Terrence J. Harding" is written on the signature line and the written signature is "Terry Harding," revealing to the reader that you are a male, and you prefer to be called "Terry" rather than "Terrence."

- You might also choose to identify your gender by using your full middle name in the signature line. Thus, "Terry Joseph Harding on the typed signature line can be signed "Terry Harding."

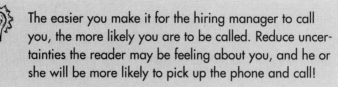

The easier you make it for the hiring manager to call you, the more likely you are to be called. Reduce uncertainties the reader may be feeling about you, and he or she will be more likely to pick up the phone and call!

- You may include titles or degrees (for example, Ph.D., C.P.A., L.P.N.) after your name, especially if they relate to your career field and will be easily recognized and understood by your target audience. You worked hard to earn them, so flaunt them!
- If you are known by your middle name rather than your first name, write it using the first initial, such as "F. William Shipley." Be careful to match the name on your resume! If your cover letter says, "William Shipley" and your resume says, "Frederick W. Shipley," the reader may be confused.

Typist Identification

Twenty years ago, a business letter that omitted the typist's initials would have been considered incomplete and incorrect. As the professional world has moved away from typewriters and adjusted to computers and word processing programs, typist identification has become less significant. So as a cover letter writer of today, do you include typist initials, or not?

This is one of those cases where you can do it the way you feel most comfortable. If your letter feels somehow in error without the initials, include them. They are no longer a necessary part of business correspondence, however, and you may omit them completely if you wish.

If you do choose to include typist initials, place them flush with the left margin, two lines below the signature block. Type the initials in lower case, as in "bjs" for "Brandt Joseph Schurenberg."

The Enclosure Line

The enclosure line simply notes to the reader that another document (in this case, your resume) is enclosed with your letter. To do this, simply type the word "Enclosure" flush left and two lines below the signature block or the typist identification line if you have included one. If you have more than one enclosure, simply use the plural, "Enclosures."

The enclosure line is another fading part of business correspondence today, and you may or may not choose to include it on your cover letter. Most hiring officials will not bristle if the enclosure line is missing, but if you prefer to be especially formal and correct, or if you know that the potential employer is a stickler for perfection, you should remember to include it at the very bottom of your cover letter.

CHAPTER SUMMARY

In this chapter, you learned to write effective closing statements that give your cover letter a strong finish.

CHAPTER 8

The Ad Response Letter

In this chapter, you will learn to write a two-column cover letter in response to a job advertisement. This type of letter captures the attention of hiring managers because of its no-nonsense style and focus on their needs.

READING AND RESPONDING TO JOB ADS

In many cases, the cover letter you write will be in response to a publicly advertised position. You may have discovered the ad on a bulletin board at work, in a newspaper or trade publication, or, as more and more job seekers are finding, on the Internet.

While most job seekers tend to answer such ads by sending off their more generalized traditional letter, you can stand apart from the others by writing a cover letter that gets right to the needs of that particular employer. How? By using the advertisement to clue you in on exactly what qualifications the employer is looking for!

To write a cover letter that stands out from the countless others sent in response, you must know how to read between the lines of what the job advertisement says. Let's examine a typical job ad and see what kind of information we might glean from it:

Accounting Position

F/T opportunity for dependable individual to be a part of a fast-paced
printing distribution co. Responsibilities include all facets of
general accounting with focus on accounts receivable, accounts payable,
and invoicing. Required skills include 2-5 yrs. accounting exp.,
knowledge of Windows 98, Microsoft Word & Excel. Experience with job
costing a plus. Competitive salary & excellent benefits. Please fax
resume with salary requirements to (555) 555-2909; email at
<u>pwinton@printfo.com</u> or mail resume to Attn. Patti Winton, Printfo
Systems, P.O. Box 90019, Claremont, MN 54029.

This ad seems simple enough to decipher. Yet if you understand the perspective of the hiring manager who wrote it, it will help you to know how to write a cover letter that will hit the important points the hardest.

Keep the perspective of the hiring manager in mind when formulating your cover letter in response to a job advertisement. Refer to the previous example as you study the following seven rules.

Consider Every Word Important

The first rule of thumb to follow when reading job ads is to ask yourself this question: "Why are they telling me this?" As you may know, placing ads in almost any publication is quite expensive. Every word the company puts in the ad is costing them money. So each word they bother to print is probably pretty important, right?

When you read it from that perspective, even commonplace words like "dependable" and "fast-paced" that may have given you little pause should make you stop and consider just why they chose to include these words and not others. If those words were important to the company in writing the ad, they should be important to you in writing your letter.

Assume That What Comes First Is Most Important

When writing a job ad, most employers will list the most vital qualifications first, then move down the line to those qualifications that are desired but not required, as in "experience with job costing a plus."

When writing your cover letter, respond to the requirements in the same way: most important first, less important later in the letter.

Take Advantage of the Company Name

If the job advertisement reveals the name of the company that is doing the hiring, use that knowledge to your full advantage. Look up the company's Web site, or do other research (see chapter 14) to discern the latest goings-on with the organization. Referring to company specifics in your cover letter makes an outstanding first impression, setting you apart from the scores of other cover letter writers who send in standard format letters with no regard to the particular company to which they are being sent.

It is sometimes possible to do company research even if you're given only a P.O. Box rather than a company name. Call the local post office that handles that address and cite the Freedom of Information Act. By law, they must tell you who placed the ad in the newspaper.

Feel Confident About a 75 Percent Match

When employers write job ads, they typically write a wish list, including skills that they know would be nice for a candidate to have, but realistically, they probably won't get in most candidates. It is a mistake to assume that if you don't have 100 percent of all the skills they list in the ad, you won't be considered for the job.

Don't Give Specific Salary Information Unless Absolutely Necessary

Many job ads ask you to talk about your salary history or salary requirements. This helps the hiring managers decide whether you fit into their financial parameters for the job. It puts them at the advantage when it comes time for salary negotiations, however, so it is better to leave all salary information off of your cover letter completely. Consider this: If you list a salary that is higher than the employer wanted to pay, you will price yourself out of the job before you even get a chance to the interview. The screeners may just toss your nice resume in the trash. If you list a salary that is too low, you may still get the job offer, but at a much lower salary than they might have otherwise paid.

So how do you avoid their questions?

Although you should make some mention of the salary issue if it has been requested in the job ad, try being as vague as possible with your answer. Never reveal your dollar-for-dollar salary history or expectations, and always speak in terms of salary ranges. Some suggestions:

- If the ad asks for your salary expectations, say this: "My salary expectations are flexible," or, "my salary expectations are negotiable." This way you've addressed the question without revealing any numbers that can be used against you at offer time. Remember, there will be time to negotiate your terms later. For now, you simply want to make it to the interview.

- If the ad asks for salary history, say this: "My salary history has been consistently progressive as I have been promoted to increasingly responsible positions." Never list specific salary figures you've earned through the course of your career. These numbers do nothing to promote your cause and may hurt you during negotiations.

- If the ad *insists* on specific details of your salary, use ranges to give yourself a broader chance of being within the parameters they are looking for. Most job seekers should use a range of about 10K, such as, "My salary expectations are in the $30K to $40K range."

- An easy way to offer limited salary information with an even broader range is to say, "My salary is in the low six figures," or, "I'm looking for a salary in the upper five figures." These vague parameters give you plenty of room to maneuver at negotiation time.

 Don't let your low-end figure be any lower than your absolute bottom line salary that you'd accept for that job.

Call the Company and Ask for a Written Job Description for the Advertised Opening

A written description will probably provide you with many more details than the published version provided. These details will help you to target your letter to the requirements of the job.

Send Your Resume As the Ad Requests

Job ads might specify that you send in your resume by e-mail, by fax, through the mail, or even that you apply in person. Whatever the ads states you should do, follow the rules as they are set forth. If you are given several choices on how to send your resume, as is the case with the ad shown earlier, you may choose any of the options, whichever you are most comfortable with.

> Whenever a company invites you to drop off a resume in person, take them up on their offer! This is a terrific opportunity to meet key players in your job search, and may result in an on-the-spot job interview.

No matter how you send your cover letter and resume package, you may want to follow up with a quick telephone call to verify its safe arrival. Don't attempt to turn this phone call into a sell-job, however, or you risk the appearance of desperation. Human resources personnel don't appreciate callers who try to finagle a job interview out of a simple follow-up call. If the job ad states, "no phone calls," you should consider forgoing the phone call altogether.

> Some experts advise that a hard copy sent through the mail is still the most reliable and risk-free way to send your resume. Of course, when time is of the essence, you may need to rely on the speed of a fax or e-mail.

WRITING YOUR AD RESPONSE COVER LETTER

The written job advertisement offers you the perfect opportunity to tailor your cover letter to the specific needs of the company and the particular qualifications of the job at hand. If your skills and background are a good fit for the job, you should have plenty to say about how your skills match their needs. Since you can hit the point so precisely, why waste time with flowery language and unnecessary information?

A two-column cover letter allows you to address each job requirement specifically, and keeps your letter direct and to the point. Set up your cover letter like this:

Patti Winton
Printfo Systems
P.O. Box 90019
Claremont, MN 54029

Dear Ms. Winton,

This responds to your advertisement in the *Sun-Times* for the accounting position at Printfo Systems. As you can see, my background and skills are an excellent match for your requirements:

Your Requirements	My Qualifications
Dependable individual	4 years as Accounting Associate at DataTech, a mid-size technology company; excellent attendance record.
Focus on AR, AP, and invoicing	4 years of AR and AP; 2 years invoicing. Created and implemented simpler invoicing system that saved unnecessary steps and reduced processing time by 25%.
2 years accounting experience	4 years progressively responsible general accounting experience. Chosen to supervise clerk staff during rush season. Known for consistently low error rate and excellent communication skills with management and staff.
Knowledge of Windows 98, Word, and Microsoft Excel	Very familiar with Windows 98, MS Word, and MS Excel; used them on daily basis.

There are other areas of accomplishment in my background that may be of interest to you. I will call you early next week to discuss the possibility of a personal meeting. Or, you are welcome to reach me at 555-555-9086.

Sincerely,

Kiera Anderson

Kiera Anderson

THE TWO-COLUMN APPROACH, PIECE BY PIECE
The Opening

Your two-column letter should open succinctly and with direct reference to the newspaper ad you are responding to. It should be no more than two or three lines, stating simply that you are responding to their newspaper advertisement, and that your skills are an excellent match for the requirements they listed in the ad.

It's important to get the name of the person to whom you need to address your letter. When responding to an ad, gathering that information can be more of a challenge. Some job ads, for example, simply ask you to send your resume to a P.O. Box number. If this is the case, try these sleuthing techniques:

- If you know the name of the company but not the name of the person to whom you'll be sending the letter, gather all the clues you have so far to see if you might learn more. Do you know the name of the department the letter will go to? Which division is the job most likely in? Do you have a job title but no name, as in "Please send to: District Sales Manager, Monasto Corp."? The more information you start out with, the easier it is to find a name.

- If you have a company name and a job title, your problem is easily remedied. Simply call the company receptionist and ask for the spelling of the person's name. Need an excuse for asking? Just tell her you plan to send that person something, and you need to know the correct name and address.

- If you have the company name alone, you might use the clues you have from the ad to guess which department or division is doing the hiring. If it is an accounting position, for example, the job will likely be in the accounting department. You might try calling the department manager and asking if the position in the ad would be located in that department. Then explain that you are attempting to send a resume and cover letter, and you'd like a name to address your letter to.

Be prepared! You can use this opportunity to network a bit with potentially important hiring managers. Who knows where a personal conversation might lead? Have a list of additional questions ready that show your knowledge of the field and showcase how well your skills match their needs.

- If you have no luck locating a name for your letter, you have no choice but to use a broad, generic salutation. Try to steer clear of worn-out phrases like "To Whom It May Concern." Pay attention not to sound sexist, either, as with, "Dear Sir." "Dear Sir or Madam" sounds too stiff and stuffy. So what *can* you use? If all you have is a P.O. Box number, how about "Dear Hiring Manager"? You might also choose to avoid a salutation altogether.

The Body

The body of the letter is set up in two columns, with "Your Requirements" at the head of the first column, and "My Qualifications" at the head of the second column. The first column lists the company's requirements as they are stated in the job ad. The second column addresses each requirement with a matching skill or job experience that meets or beats the requirement.

Start with the requirements that the ad has listed first. These are usually the most highly desired job skills, and thus will attract the most attention. List every requirement that the ad mentions. If you can fit everything on one page, list each requirement separately to give yourself space to address each one in detail. If there are too many requirements to list separately on one page, group a few related requirements together as the writer did in the previous example.

What If I Don't Meet Some of the Listed Requirements for the Job?

Don't directly mention any requirements that you don't meet. If they ask for six years of experience and you only have four, don't assume that they will let it slide by. Your letter may be reviewed by a personnelist, who is following guidelines to exclude anyone who doesn't meet the basic requirements.

If you don't meet a requirement, handle it in one of two ways:

1. Don't mention the requirement at all if you think you can get away with it. Maybe they won't even notice that you didn't mention one particular job qualification because you've matched all the others so well.

2. Mention the job requirement that you lack, but use ambiguous language to blur the picture a bit. For example, if you fail to meet a requirement for number of years of experience, use words like "several" or "extensive" instead of exact numbers to soften the shortfall.

Use Those Accomplishments!

Don't forget to prove the strengths of your skills by noting your on-the-job accomplishments, as the letter writer in the earlier example did. By mentioning her improved invoicing system and the fact that she was chosen to supervise during the busy season, the letter writer in the example let her achievements work for her to demonstrate how she could succeed in the new position.

It is important to avoid simply repeating the requirements nearly word-for word in both columns, as in:

Your Requirements	My Qualifications
Dependable individual	Very dependable
Focus on AR, AP, and invoicing	Strong background in AR, AP, and invoicing
2 years accounting experience	2+ years accounting experience
Knowledge of Windows 98, Word, and Microsoft Excel	Strong knowledge of Windows 98, Word, and Microsoft Excel

This tells the reader nothing interesting about your skills, and has a serious charm deficit. You may start your sentence with a direct comparison to the stated requirements, but be sure to follow with a few brief details or examples that give credibility to your claim.

Your Requirements	My Qualifications
Dependable Individual	Solid work history demonstrates loyalty and dependability, including 3 years as *Accounting Specialist* with *Southern Ohio College.*

I held this 30 hr/week Accounting Specialist position while attending college full-time. |
| Focus on AR, AP, and Invoicing | Gained A/R expertise as Coordinator of Southern Ohio College's Managed Installment Program.

Oversaw A/P portion of Campus Co-op program, involving over 120 student employees.

Continually evaluated student accounts for outstanding debt, and invoiced students on a timely basis. Reduced outstanding accounts by 20% in 4 month period. |
| 2 years accounting experience | 3 years solid accounting experience with broad background in A/P, A/R, and invoicing. Developed excellent oral and written communication skills through interactions with students and administrators. |
| Knowledge of Windows 98, Word, and Microsoft Excel. | Proficient with PC based software packages such as Windows 98, Excel, Word, Access, and Graphics. |

The Close

Your two-column letter should close as succinctly as it has been written. The closing paragraph should mention that there is more to discuss, and suggest a personal meeting or interview. As in the traditional cover letter, you should take the initiative with the follow-up call, telling the employer that you will call "later in the week" or "early next week" to discuss the possibilities.

 Don't forget to include your 10-digit phone number on the cover letter as well. You never know who will be so inspired by your letter that they will want to call you immediately!

 Be thorough and include your area code on the cover letter along with your telephone number. Many urban areas are divided into several area codes. Why take a chance on something so simple?

Two-Column Cover Letter Do's and Don'ts

DO keep it to one page. Anything more takes away the best feature of this letter: its no-frills crispness.

DO read the ad carefully! Don't miss important requirements and neglect to address them in your letter.

DON'T simply repeat the exact requirement as stated in your "My Qualifications" column. This tells the reader nothing about what you can actually do. Spice things up with details that back up your claims.

DO be sure to include a thorough history of your career: the name of your previous or current company, the years you were employed there, your job titles, and so on. It can be easy to forget these things when you are addressing specific requirements. Remember, however, that the reader will have a copy of your resume to refer to if there is a need to fill in any forgotten details.

DO be sure to match your skills directly to the needs of the company. Consider each of the requirements attentively, and take care to list the skills you have that directly fulfill those requirements.

CHAPTER SUMMARY

In this chapter, you learned to write a cover letter in response to a job advertisement that impresses the reader with a no-nonsense, two-column approach.

CHAPTER 9

The Cover Letter to Recruiters and Search Firms

In this chapter, you will learn how recruiters and employment agencies can help in your job search and how you can write a cover letter that compels them to consider you for their clients' job openings.

Recruiters and search firms have become commonplace in today's job search process. Middle managers, technical workers, specialists, upper-level managers, and many others receive job propositions from recruiters on a regular basis. These recruiters are on assignment for a company, looking to fill a position with a certain type of employee who matches a defined set of qualifications.

SEARCH FIRM BASICS

Many job seekers balk at the idea of using a recruiter or employment agency to help them in their job search. Some feel that these companies lack integrity and are out to make a buck instead of find satisfying jobs for their customers. Others don't like to turn over the control of their search to someone else.

Using recruiters can be a positive experience, though, as long as you are savvy to the way the system works. It can be a great way to get the inside scoop on positions that might not be advertised to the general public. Best of all, it's usually free of charge, so what do you have to lose? Follow these guidelines for using recruiters successfully:

- Never pay a fee to a recruiter, unless you are a first-time job seeker. In most cases, the hiring company pays the service fee, not the job seeker. Don't ever pay a fee up front!

- Don't give exclusivity to any firm. Some recruiters ask you to sign a form that gives them the right to work with you exclusively. Don't sign it—let as many recruiters help you in your job search as you can get!

- Never tell a recruiter where you have interviewed, unless that recruiter sets up the interview for you. Otherwise, he or she can use this information to send other people out for that job, which can hurt your chances of getting hired.

Recruiters are known by several names: headhunters, executive search firms, staffing agencies, or personnel consultants, to name a few. Despite the plethora of names, most firms fall into one of just three distinct groups: employment agencies, contingency firms, and retainer firms.

Employment Agencies

Employment agencies most often find positions for entry-level through middle-management job candidates. Frequently, they specialize in clerical personnel, administrative workers, accounting staff, technical specialists, or industrial workers. They might also handle various office positions for entry-level workers that don't require specific administrative skills, such as inventory workers or registration assistants.

Employment agencies often deal with a large volume of positions simultaneously, some temporary or part-time, some temp-to-hire, others full-time and permanent. They are usually listed in the local Yellow Pages, and many are national firms with offices and contacts across the United States.

In most cases, employment agencies are paid by the employer who makes use of their service, and so the job candidate is not required to pay a fee. In rare cases, the job candidate is required to pay a fee to the employment agency upon acceptance of a position with an agency-contacted company.

Contingency Firms

Contingency firms usually handle jobs in the middle-salary ranges, but the positions they handle can range from entry level to upper management. They have a lower volume of traffic than employment agencies, and therefore can devote more specialized attention to their job candidates and client companies. They work to find employee matches for local and national companies with jobs to fill. The contingency firm doesn't get paid until the match is made.

Retainer Firms

Retainer firms deal almost exclusively with upper-level management positions in the higher salary ranges. These firms work on retainer for companies that have high-level positions to fill. Retainer firms typically conduct searches for job candidates across the nation or internationally.

 No matter which type of recruiting firm you are associated with, remember that their client companies pay their salaries, not you. This means that they are quite concerned with pleasing the client companies, and less concerned with pleasing *you*.

Specialized Agencies

The current trend in recruiting firms, especially employment agencies and contingency firms, is toward more specialized services and a narrower focus. Generalist agencies are being replaced by firms that specialize in specific job functions, such as accounting, technical, medical, or industrial. These can help you in your job search to identify which agencies will offer you the most opportunities for positions in your field.

Specialized agencies can be a good choice for a job seeker with specific skills or well-defined job goals, because they are familiar with the industry or field and have many contacts there.

FINDING A RECRUITER

Look in your local Yellow Pages for a listing of employment agencies in your area. You will likely find pages of firms that offer staffing services in a variety of shapes and sizes. Pick the employment agencies that suit your background and needs, and list them on a sheet of paper. These will be the target of your cover letter.

If your experience is more at the level of a contingency or retainer search firm, you will have to do a bit more digging to find names of firms that can handle your needs. One excellent resource is called *The Directory of Executive Recruiters,* which can be found at most local libraries in the reference section. *The Directory of Executive Recruiters* is updated annually, and offers thorough information on recruiting firms across the nation. It is divided into contingency and retainer sections, and allows you to search for firms alphabetically or by a number of criteria such as geographic location, job function, industry, or recruiter specialty.

Another good option for finding executive recruiting firms is to log on to the Internet and type in the keywords "Executive Recruiter Directories." You'll find a huge listing of recruiter directories, some with specific focus on particular employment or geographic areas. Many of these databases allow you to download full contact information for the executive recruiters in your specialty.

CRAFTING YOUR RECRUITER-ORIENTED COVER LETTER

Once you have chosen a list of employment agencies or executive recruiters with whom you'd like to work, it is time to begin crafting your cover letter. The cover letter to recruiters is formatted in much the same way as your traditional cover letter, yet it differs on some important points.

Consider your audience when drafting the contents of your cover letter. How many cover letters do you think a recruiter reads in a single day? Professional recruiters are some of the savviest hiring managers out there, and it isn't easy to impress someone who has seen it all. Treat them with respect, and you might find yourself on the inside of one of the most powerful job hunt networks available today.

Follow these two general rules to keep you from going astray:

1. **Be brief.** Busy recruiters won't accommodate wordiness.

2. **Respect their know-how.** Don't try to inflate your skills or over-state your experience. To a seasoned eye, your puffery will be transparent, and your credibility will be shot.

> Recruiters have great connections. They have forged relationships with countless hiring managers whom you might love to meet, so write your letter to impress!

How Recruiters Read Cover Letters

Recruiters work hard for their client companies to find job candidates who match a set of qualifications for a specific position. When they receive cover letters and resumes, they are looking less at the personality of the job candidate, and more at specific skill sets. This is quite different from the corporate hiring managers who are filling positions within their own companies, and are especially concerned with finding someone whose personal characteristics match their working environment.

Thus, when writing your cover letters to recruiters, focus on a clear presentation of your job interests, skills, and experience.

What to Include

The cover letter to a recruiting firm should contain the following elements:

- Your return address
- Date
- Address of recruiting firm
- Salutation
- Opening paragraph
- Your job objective
- A brief summary of your qualifications
- One or two examples of a particular accomplishment with result
- Your phone number (and e-mail address, if applicable)
- Statement of appreciation
- Closing and signature

THE OPENING

Your introductory paragraph should be brief and to the point. Don't try to win the recruiter over with an attempt at flattery, humor, a quote from a business guru, a line from a poem, or any other endeavor meant to surprise or charm. Recruiters want to know what skills and experience you have to offer, and they want to know it up front.

Start your letter with something like this:

- "Among your many clients might be one or two who are looking for a [senior-level financial executive]."
- "I am currently seeking a position as a [mid-level manufacturing manager]. Please consider me for any executive search assignments requiring someone with my credentials."
- "I am forwarding my resume to you because I understand you specialize in light industrial placements, and may have client companies who would have interest in my [assembly-line] experience."
- "Perhaps one of your clients would have interest in my [customer service] background."
- "I am sending you my resume for your clients' consideration if there is a need for an experienced [MIS professional]."

In these examples, notice how carefully worded the bracketed job titles are. You must be careful to present your background in such a way that is neither too narrow nor too broad, so that the reader understands how to define your occupation. Be careful not to limit your prospects by choosing words that are too specific.

For example:

- Don't call yourself a "bank branch manager," call yourself a "banking professional" or someone with "bank management experience."
- Don't call yourself a "client/server systems integration specialist," call yourself an "information systems specialist" or "IT professional with expertise in client/server systems integration."

In this opening paragraph, the trick is to steer clear of company-specific job titles, and use a broader definition of your skills so that you don't get overlooked for positions you might be interested in. Think more in terms of the industry or field you are in, rather than your particular job title. You will have room for specifics in the next paragraph.

It is equally dangerous to be *too* broad with your job definition, leaving the recruiter wondering just where you might fit in. If your credentials can't be matched quite specifically to a client's job requirements, the recruiter will have a hard time selling you to that company for an interview. Try to define yourself in these ways:

- By career level (manager, administrator, specialist, supervisor, etc.)
- By field or industry (banking industry, chemical manufacturer, the purchasing field, etc.)
- By number of years of experience

These specifics help the recruiter know where you fit in to his or her schedule of open positions.

If your experience is limited to fewer than two or three years, you may find it more enhancing to use descriptors instead of numbers to describe your experience, such as, "strong background in loan administration" or "comprehensive experience in all aspects of warehouse shipping operations."

Be conscious of potential age discrimination. Any employer can calculate your approximate current age if you use specific numbers when describing your years of experience. It may be wise to describe anything over 20 years experience in less specific terms, such as "20+ years in hospital administration" or "over 20 years experience in the health care industry." You can also choose to avoid numbers altogether, by saying something like, "extensive experience in hospital administration."

THE BODY

The main portion of your search firm cover letter should begin with a brief paragraph that summarizes your background and skills. This might include educational credentials in addition to professional work experience, if your schooling is something you want to emphasize.

Be sure to stay focused on the skills and accomplishments that support your stated job objective. Avoid mentioning daily job duties that add nothing of interest to your skills set. As with all cover letters, don't write inactive phrases such as "My responsibilities included . . . " or talk about your "job description."

In your background statement, you might add a concise sentence or two about a specific accomplishment to support your statement of skills. Study the following examples for ideas:

- "I have a business degree from the University of Cincinnati, and over 10 years' experience in finance, credit, and collections. I have a strong background in financial management, servicing customer accounts, and collections activity. In fact, my persistent and thorough collections work reduced my company's quarterly bad debt rate by 35%."

- "I have a Bachelor of Architecture and a Juris Doctor. I am familiar with many community development practices including tax increment financing, development fees, exactions, capital facilities planning, and bond issues. A sample of my recent accomplishments include:

  Wrote a proposal and won a grant to build a senior/community center.

  Designed and planned the opening of a downtown business loop road."

SALARY REQUIREMENTS AND GEOGRAPHIC PREFERENCES

Two subjects that cause disagreement from the experts about whether to include them on the cover letter are geographic relocation preferences and salary requirements. Of course, if you are very open regarding salary or geographic possibilities, there is no worry about including this on your letter. It is when you specify preferences that there is cause for concern.

If you asked a recruiter to tell you what to include in your cover letter, you would probably be told to write as much detailed information as possible about your salary history and your location parameters. For example, if you aren't willing to relocate, it should be stated in your cover letter, so the recruiter knows not to waste time calling you about a job on the other side of the country. Or if your salary requirements are firm and you won't accept a position below $50,000, the recruiter knows not to bother calling you for positions that pay less.

These ideas are helpful to the recruiter, but there is some question whether they are really helpful to *you*. Should you limit yourself to letting the recruiter decide which jobs you will be put in line for and which jobs you won't? Wouldn't it be better to let the recruiter call you to give you the lowdown on the job and let *you* decide if you are interested or not?

Keep Broad Parameters

The best thing for most job candidates is to define salary and location parameters in a way that guides the recruiter to the jobs that fit best, but that doesn't knock you out of the running for other potential action. As you state your preferences, remain as broad as possible. For your geographic preference, for example, you might write that you would "like to stay in the Northeast area, if possible," or that "My family and I prefer to relocate to the PA-MD-VA tri-state area."

The salary issue can be handled the same way. A good choice for playing the middle ground on the salary issue is to offer the salary figures recruiters desire, but give it to them in a more generalized form. For example, rather than saying, "My current salary is $51,500," try something like, "My current salary is in the $50,000–$60,000 range." Using a range gives you more leeway when it comes time for negotiation, and won't narrow your parameters as severely.

A way to broaden the parameters on salary even further is to say something like, "My current salary is in the mid-five figures" or "My current salary is approaching six figures." This gives you a nice, broad $20K to $30K spread.

YOUR REASON FOR LEAVING

More debate exists over whether to include your reason for leaving your current or past position on your recruiter cover letter. Recruiters like to have this information, of course, so that they can know the circumstances surrounding your job change.

In most cases, I would recommend that your reason for leaving be left off the letter altogether. No matter how well justified your reason may be, it always reads as a slight negative, simply because there are negative undertones to leaving any job.

If you feel it is important to include your reasons, then do so quickly and move on. Don't dwell on this area. Say something like, "Due to a recent restructuring at XYZ, my current position has been eliminated. I am looking forward to new opportunities where I can put my 11 years of training and development to work."

THE CLOSE

Close your cover letter with a quick statement of appreciation for the recruiter's time and a note on how you can be reached. As opposed to the traditional cover letter, you may choose to give the responsibility for the follow-up phone call to the recipient of the letter. Recruiters are quite adept at being discreet, so you can feel comfortable with giving them your current work number even if your job search is confidential. If you include an e-mail address, you might opt to give your home account address to ensure privacy.

 As with all cover letters, the easier you make it for the reader to contact you, the more likely you are to get called.

Some examples of closing remarks:

> I have enclosed my resume for your review, and would greatly appreciate your consideration. I can be reached on a confidential basis during the day at (513) 555-4477, or by e-mail at Marsich @AOL.com. I look forward to the prospect from of hearing you.
>
> Sincerely,
>
> Brandyn Marengo

> Should you be conducting a search for someone with my background, I would appreciate hearing from you. I would be happy to discuss my credentials with you by phone or in a personal interview. You can reach me during the day at (719) 555-9087 on a confidential basis, or in the evenings at (719) 555-0991.
>
> Thank you for your consideration.
>
> Yours Truly,
>
> Jaime Floures

RECRUITER COVER LETTER SAMPLES

Appendix B offers several examples of complete cover letters to send to recruiters and employment agencies. Study them according to your situation, and use them as guides to create the letter that works best for you. Then plug in your own information, and combine bits and pieces of them to make your own unique composition.

CHAPTER SUMMARY

In this chapter, you learned to write a cover letter to recruiting firms that includes the important information recruiters need to know, without hurting your prospects for the broadest range of jobs.

CHAPTER 10

Giving It a Fresh Face: The Cover Letter Layout

In this chapter, you will learn how to format your letter for a professional presentation. You will also learn about paper choice, font styles, and coordinating your job search package.

Even the most perfectly written cover letter won't make it past the first cut if it doesn't have a presentable appearance. The toughest part of the sales pitch is the first impression your letter makes, and the reader's first impression is set by the look of the letter before any words are actually read.

In most cases, cover letters are up against heavy competition, and it's tough to stand out when the crowd is thick. Most cover letters, especially those written in response to a job advertisement, are being reviewed along with a stack of maybe 40 to 50 others. At best, each letter gets about a 20-second chance to win over the reader before it gets set aside. With so little time and so much competition, a letter has to catch the reader's interest in a mere glance.

COMMON FORMAT PROBLEMS THAT CREATE NEGATIVE FIRST IMPRESSIONS

Employers know immediately when a cover letter is below par. Here are some of their most common formatting criticisms:

- The cover letter is too bulky: Too much junk is crammed onto the page, so that the good stuff is buried and too troublesome to dig out.
- The page looks slipshod and sloppy, making the writer appear disorganized or lazy or both.
- Words are misused and misspelled. Grammar is poor.
- The print is smudged or faded.
- The font is too small or too fancy for comfortable reading.

APPROPRIATE LETTER FORMATS

Cover letters should be set up as standard business correspondence, using today's business protocol. Two formats prevail in the current business climate: the *full block* and the *standard block*. Either of these styles is completely acceptable for the typical cover letter. Choose the one that seems right for you.

Full Block Format

All components of the full block format—the return address, date, address, salutation, closing, signature, and enclosure lines—are flush with the left margin. No part of the letter is indented. This format has a crisp, no-nonsense appeal. The full block letter format is shown in the following example.

```
xxxxxxxxxx      (return address, if desired)
xxxxxxxxxx
xxxxxxxxxx

xxxxxxxxxx      (date)

xxxxxxxxxx      (name, title, address)
xxxxxxxxxx
xxxxxxxxxx
xxxxxxxxxx

xxxxxxxxxxxxx   (salutation)

xxxxxxxxxxxxxxxxxxxxxxxxxxxxxxxxxxxxxxxxxxxxxxxxxxxxxxxxxxxxxxxxxxxxxx
xxxxxxxxxxxxxxxxxxxxxxxxxxxxxxxxxxxxxxxxxxxxxxxxxxxxxxxxxxxxxxxxxxxxxx
xxxxxxxxxxxxxxxxxxxxxxxxxxxxxx.

xxxxxxxxxxxxxxxxxxxxxxxxxxxxxxxxxxxxxxxxxxxxxxxxxxxxxxxxxxxxxxxxxxxxxx
xxxxxxxxxxxxxxxxxxxxxxxxxxxxxxxxxxxxxxxxxxxxxxxxxxxxxxxxxxxxxxxxxxxxxx
xxxxxxxxxxxxxxxxxxxxxxxxxxxxxxxxxxxxxxxxxxxxxxxxxxxxxxxxxxxxxxxxxxxxxx
xxxxxxxxxxxxxxxxxxxxxxxxxxxxxxxxxxxxxxxxxxxxxxx.

xxxxxxxxxxxxxxxxxxxxxxxxxxxxxxxxxxxxxxxxxxxxxxxxxxxxxxxxxxxxxxxxxxxxxx
xxxxxxxxxxxxxxxxxxxxxxxxxxxxxxxxxxxxxxxxxxxxxxxxxxxxxxxxxxxxxxxxxxxxxx
xxxxxxxxxxxxxxxxxxxxxxxxxxxxxxxxxxxxxxxxxxxxxxxxxxxxxxxxxxxxxxxxxxxxxx
xxxxxxxxxxxxxxxxxxxxxxxxxxxxxxxxxxxxxxxxxx.

xxxxxxxxxxxxxxxxxxxxxxxxxxxxxxxxxxxxxxxxxxxxxxxxxxxxxxxxxxxxxxxxxxxxxx
xxxxxxxxxxxxxxxxxxxxxxxxxxxxxxxxxxxxxxxxxxxxxxxxxxxxxxxx.

xxxxxxxxxxxxxxxx    (closing)


xxxxxxxxxxxxxxxx    (signature line)

xxxxx              (enclosure line, if desired)
```

Standard Block Format

The standard block format is similar to the full block format in that all paragraphs, the salutation, and the address are flush with the left margin. It differs in that the return address and date are indented so that the longest line is flush with the letter's right margin. Also, the closing and signature lines are indented. These latter two may be indented as follows:

- Flush with the right margin
- Five spaces to the right of the center of the page
- Centered on the page

Be sure that the first letters of the closing line and the signature line are vertically aligned. See the following example.

```
                                    (return address)    xxxxxxxxxxxx
                                                        xxxxxxxxxxxx
                                                        xxxxxxxxxxxx

xxxxxxxxxxxx            (date)

xxxxxxxxxxxxxxxxxx      (name, title, address)
xxxxxxxxxxxxxxxxxx
xxxxxxxxxxxxxxxxxx

xxxxxxxxxxxxxxxxxxxx    (salutation)

xxxxxxxxxxxxxxxxxxxxxxxxxxxxxxxxxxxxxxxxxxxxxxxxxxxxxxxxxxxxxxxxxxxx
xxxxxxxxxxxxxxxxxxxxxxxxxxxxxxxxxxxxxxxxxxxxxxxxxxxxxxxxxxxxxxxxxxxx
xxxxxxxxxxxxxxxxxxxxxxxxxxxxxxxxxxxxxxxxxxx.

xxxxxxxxxxxxxxxxxxxxxxxxxxxxxxxxxxxxxxxxxxxxxxxxxxxxxxxxxxxxxxxxxxxx
xxxxxxxxxxxxxxxxxxxxxxxxxxxxxxxxxxxxxxxxxxxxxxxxxxxxxxxxxxxxxxxxxxxx
xxxxxxxxxxxxxxxxxxxxxxxxxxxxxxxxxxxxxxxxxxxxxxxxxxxxxxxxxxxxxxxxxxxx
xxxxxxxxxxxxxxxxxxxxx.

xxxxxxxxxxxxxxxxxxxxxxxxxxxxxxxxxxxxxxxxxxxxxxxxxxxxxxxxxxxxxxxxxxxx
xxxxxxxxxxxxxxxxxxxxxxxxxxxxxxxxxxxxxxxxxxxxxxxxxxxxxxxxxxxxxxxxxxxx
xxxxxxxxxxxxxxxxxxxxxxxxxxxxxxxxxxxxxxxxxxxxxxxxxxxxxxxxxxxxxxxxxxxx
xxxxxxxxxxxxxxxxxxxxxxxxxxxxxxxx.

xxxxxxxxxxxxxxxxxxxxxxxxxxxxxxxxxxxxxxxxxxxxxxxxxxxxxxxxxxxxxxxxxxxx
xxxxxxxxxxxxxxxxxxxxxxxxxxxxxxxxxxxxxxxxxxxxxxxxxxxxxxxxxxxxx.

                       (closing)                xxxxxxxxxxxx


                       (signature line)         xxxxxxxxxxxx

xxxxxx         (enclosure line, if desired)
```

Indented Paragraphs

Some business correspondence is still written in the more old-fashioned modified block style, in which the first line of every paragraph is indented. In all other ways, this style is identical to the standard block format. Although some writers still use the indented paragraphs, they are considered more appropriate for personal correspondence, and are thought to be too informal for conservative business letters.

PRINTING YOUR COVER LETTER

Word processors have now become so commonplace that it is expected that your cover letter will be written on one. Letters produced on old-fashioned typewriters are considered to be inferior in print quality, not to mention outdated and archaic. Even if you don't own a word processor, you would be wise to beg or borrow your way to the use of one so you can give your cover letter the professional appearance that only a word processor can give. Public libraries and community college campuses often have word processors available for such uses.

It is important to recognize that not all printers can give you a professional look. Old-fashioned dot matrix, thermal, or near letter quality (NLQ) printers will give your letter an outdated look that will give the reader the sense that you are technologically behind the times. These printers also work against you if the company uses a scanner, since many scanners cannot read the output of NLQ, thermal, or dot matrix printers.

 If at all possible, print your cover letter on a laser or laser-quality printer.

Choosing the Font

The font, or typeface, that you choose can make a big difference in the impression your cover letter makes on its reader. It sets the mood and tone of the entire letter.

Your cover letter should be written in a font that looks professional, is easy to read, and doesn't call attention to itself. This is not the medium through which you should express your creative urges or make the statement that you are a bold risk taker. Instead, use fonts that suggest a firm grasp of today's business practices. Any of these fonts are good choices for a cover letter. Choose your favorite:

Arial

Bookman

Calisto

Times New Roman

Verdana

Book Antiqua

Stay away from fancy fonts that are fun to look at for a short period, but are overwhelming in a cover letter (except perhaps in the letterhead). Some examples are:

Comic Sans MS

Impact

Lucida Handwriting

COPPERPLATE GOTHIC

A Few Rules About Fonts and Typefaces

Remember that a well-written cover letter has a professional, inviting appearance. It should be traditional, neat, and easy on the eyes. There should be plenty of white space on the page to create an uncluttered style that is pleasing to the reader. Note the following tips on how to give your letter the most appealing look:

1. Avoid heavy, bold typeface for the body of your cover letter. Bold can smudge or blur when being faxed or copied, which will do irreparable damage to your presentation.

2. Script typefaces that have the appearance of handwriting can be a tempting choice for a letter writer who wants to set a more casual tone; however, script is simply not appropriate for this type of formal business correspondence, except for use in the letterhead.

3. Within sentences, don't overuse the **bold** or <u>underline</u> option in attempting to give a statement more impact. Too many of these merely distract the reader from the point being made and give your letter the appearance of immaturity. Your statements should be worded in such a way that the impact is written into the sentence.

4. Avoid the use of exclamation points!! They appear amateurish, or make you appear overzealous.

5. You may use the *italics* key to direct emphasis on a word when the placement of emphasis might not otherwise be clear, but you shouldn't have to resort to this tactic more than once throughout the letter. If there is a problem with emphasis, you might need to rephrase the statement.

6. Stick to only one font choice for your letter. More than one font can look jumbled and messy and will confuse computerized scanning programs.

7. Don't attempt to add zing to your letter through the use of clip-art images. Borders and scrolls are not in keeping with the conservative, professional look you want.

Creating a Letterhead

You may wish to create your own letterhead at the top of your cover letter paper. If done right, this can look quite professional, and gives you a chance to put your creative energies to use. Your letterhead should be in the same or complementary typeface as the body of your letter, although you may want to make the font size larger than your letter text. You may also choose to use bold, underline, or italics to make it visually interesting, but beware of the negative effect these can have on computerized scanners. Some examples:

F. Ward Blair

678 Irwin Lane, Lakota KY 46007
(606) 555-3838

HANDLING MULTIPLE PAGES

If your cover letter ends up running onto two pages, your second page should not have a letterhead like the first. Instead, type your name, address, and telephone number across the top for the sake of easy reference, like so:

Lesley Whisner 24 Carol Way Oldham, VA 21223 (670) 555-9097

Then put a page number at the bottom of the page in case your papers should get shuffled about and perhaps a page number on the first page as well. Remember the all-important cover letter rule, however: Briefer is better. If your cover letter runs onto two pages, the hiring manager may decide it isn't worth his time to read it.

> Never use both sides of the paper. If your letter gets sent through a fax or copier, the back portion will likely be forgotten.

YOUR COORDINATED LETTER CAMPAIGN

Your cover letter and resume should be printed on the same-color paper, using the same font type. All future letters should match in font and paper color, so that the entire batch of correspondence looks well-planned. This includes reference lists, thank-you letters, and other follow-up correspondence. All should be coordinated to give you a distinctive, consistent look.

Paper Choice

In today's world of electronic mail and fax machines, choosing the right paper for your cover letter hardly seems important. Who is going to see it in its original form anyway?

In actuality, the person reading your cover letter is probably going to deal with it in hard copy form at some point during the consideration process, so you might as well have the most impressive copy in front of him or her. In other words, no matter how else you might have sent your cover letter to the company, follow it up with an original hard copy by mail. This way, if the fax machine has blurred half your text, or the e-mail reformatted your letter beyond recognition, the employer will at least get a look at your letter as it was originally intended.

The hard copy you send should be printed on white or ivory-colored paper, with a quality 24# weight. The heavier bond paper makes a better presentation, and leaves the impression that you are a person who cares about details. Running your letter off on standard copier paper implies that you weren't savvy enough to know better, or that you were in a rush and didn't care enough about the potential job to do your letter up right.

Envelopes

The envelopes you use should match the paper of your resume and cover letter, so the whole look is coordinated and professional. You don't want to look like you ran out of one color and had to use a mismatch, or that you aren't sharp enough to spot such a stark error as mismatched paper color.

How to Address Your Envelopes

Let's say an employer sits down at his desk just as his mail is being delivered. In the stack are 30 envelopes, and yours is among them. How do you make sure yours is compelling enough to get opened?

- Use both name and title when addressing the envelope. Some managers assume that mail addressed to "Director, Marketing Division" is probably junk mail not worth reading. If you don't know both the name and title, call the company and ask. You don't need to identify yourself; simply say that you are sending something in the mail, and ask for the information you need.

- Even if you know the name and title, you will not impress the reader if you've spelled the name wrong. Don't guess! Even simple names like Smith and Wilson can be spelled different ways.

- Don't attempt to persuade your intended reader to open the envelope by writing "confidential" or "personal" on it. This is the equivalent of the junk mail you receive that tries to influence you with such things as, "Dated material enclosed!" or "Important information inside." It doesn't fool you, and it won't fool the hiring manager, either. In fact, if he *does* open the envelope and find that you were conning him, he won't be amused.

- A good way to ensure that your letter gets read is to hand-write your envelopes. Many employers find a neatly written envelope slightly intriguing. It tends to stand out from the stack of affixed-label junk mail that pervades their daily mail supply. Just be sure to be neat. Envelopes are cheap—if you mess up, don't cross it out. Get a new envelope, and start again.

CHAPTER SUMMARY

In this chapter, you learned about the layout of your cover letter and how to use a format that gives your letter a sharp, professional image.

CHAPTER 11

Effective Writing Techniques

In this chapter, you will learn to use simple and effective writing techniques that give your cover letter polish and flair.

Employers look for strong communication skills in job candidates for a broad spectrum of positions. Employees of all levels must be able to write reports, compose business letters, and put together sensible e-mails, memos, and faxes. A deficit in written communication skills hampers the ability of any employee to deal effectively with clients, co-workers, managers, and staff. When communication breaks down, productivity suffers, sales decrease, workers begin to grumble, and discord gains a steady foothold.

No wonder employers read cover letters with an eye not only for what is said, but for how *well* it is said. They know that if a cover letter is written well, the job candidate possesses the written communication skills that will help him or her be successful on the job.

STYLE

Style is that indefinable something that gives your letter panache and charm. It elevates your letter from dry correspondence to something interesting, something that makes the reader take notice. Style is about precision, well-chosen words, an attractive format, and a logical flow. It makes the reader feel that the writer used good judgment and careful planning to compose a pleasing, informative, and concisely written letter.

It isn't always easy to take the ideas in your head and translate them onto paper in a way that transcends the typical. Try using the following tips to help you write a cover letter with flair.

Use Action Verbs

Some cover letters seem to have all the life sapped out of them by an overly dry and rote recitation of duties and responsibilities from past jobs. In today's world of 30-second commercials and quick sound bytes, readers have little patience with letters that drag them slowly through two minutes of boredom.

Your letter needs a little pizzazz in the form of verbs that give the reader a sense of action. Action verbs, of course, demonstrate activity and give your letter power by showing how you make things happen. They add interesting details to your background, giving the reader something concrete to grasp on to.

Use active verbs that end in "-ed" to show what you have done. For example, say "I promoted a new line of products" rather than "I was responsible for promoting a new line of products." Or write "I designed a marketing brochure" rather than "My duties included designing a marketing brochure." The "-ed" ending gives the impression that you completed the project successfully.

As you write your cover letter, refer to the list of action verbs in Appendix D. Plug them in wherever your letter could use more detail.

 Make sure to show the reader what you *did*, not what your job description says somebody *should* do.

Shorter Is Better

The shorter the sentence, the stronger the punch! As you write, try to keep each sentence to no more than about 20 words—anything longer should probably be broken into two sentences. Shorter sentences break your thoughts and ideas into bite-sized bits and make your letter easier for a weary reader to digest.

The same principle that works for sentences works for paragraphs, too. (Chalk it up to the "briefer is better" school of thought.) Long paragraphs overwhelm the reader by their sheer bulk and impenetrable appearance. A good rule of thumb is to keep every paragraph under five sentences.

 If you suddenly find yourself with one big bulging paragraph, don't panic and over-edit. Simply look for logical breaks in thoughts, and divide your cumbersome paragraph into several more manageable pieces.

Cadence

Take care that your sentences have a natural flow from one to the next. Avoid a choppy style where each sentence begins with the same word, is the same length, or sounds sing-song. Read your letter aloud to yourself. Does it have a comfortable, relaxed tone and a pleasant cadence? If so, great! This is the sign of a well-written cover letter. If not, look for sentences that can be rearranged a bit to vary their structure and their sound.

Avoid Obscure Words

It's great to use a sizable vocabulary to add breadth to your letter. Using a variety of words helps you showcase your expertise and intelligence. Be cautious, however. Overusing large and obscure words can make your reader uncomfortable. There's no point in writing a letter that your reader can't understand. Never be tempted to use a fancy word when a familiar one will do just as well.

Watch the Technical Jargon

Consider your audience when sending letters that involve highly technical fields. If the cover letter you are sending is the first contact with the company, or especially if it's being sent to the human resources or personnel department, it is likely to be screened by non-technical people who may be stymied by technical jargon that they don't understand.

Save your technical details for letters addressed to fellow technical people who not only understand your technical references, but will feel a letter is incomplete without them.

Avoid Acronyms that May Stymie Your Audience

Don't assume that your reader knows what your acronyms stand for. Every company and every industry has its everyday acronyms but to outsiders, these can be cryptic. What has become everyday lingo for you may be so much alphabet soup for the reader. Leave acronyms out of your cover letter unless they are broadly familiar.

Don't Use the Same Word Multiple Times

It happens to the best of us. We latch on to a word that works particularly well in a certain place, so we use it again and again until it becomes annoyingly obvious. Try using your word processor's thesaurus for new ideas to spice up your letter with a little variety.

Watch the Emphasis Words

Some writers, in an attempt to intensify any and every statement, will overuse emphasis words, such as the word "very." For example: "I am *very* interested in the position, and would *very* much appreciate your consideration. I have a *very* strong background in sales management, and my sales figures have been *very* successful for the past three years."

Rather than using emphasis words like "very" to intensify adjectives, try using adjectives that are strong in themselves. For example, the previous statement would have more impact if written as,

"I am enthusiastic about the position and would appreciate your consideration for the job. My background in sales management is exceedingly strong, and my sales figures have been solidly successful for the past three years."

TONE

Experts give differing advice on the "perfect" tone for a cover letter. Some say the proper cover letter is ultra-formal, while others lean toward a relaxed and casual letter. Without one hard and fast rule to guide you, it isn't always easy to know what kind of style to adopt. And since you don't usually know the personality of the person who will be reading your letter, it is impossible to know what will please.

Since there are so many variables beyond your control, your best bet is to choose the middle ground: Write a cover letter in a conversational tone that leans toward the formal. Avoid a rigidly formal tone, as this removes all charm and zest. Also avoid being chummy or overly familiar, even if you know the recipient well. You don't want to look like you're cashing in on your friendship to hit him or her up for a job. Let your personality and charisma shine through, yet maintain a respectful and professional tone throughout.

Watch the "I" Word

Many cover letter writers mistakenly write their letter to match the tense and tone of the resume. Resumes typically omit the pronoun "I," and implied short words such as "a" and "the" to give the resume a more stick-to-the-facts feel. While this austerity is appealing on a resume, it has less of a place on the cover letter. A good cover letter should give the reader a little taste of your personality . . . tough to do when writing in the strict telegraphic style of a resume.

Adopt a tone that is friendly yet professional by using the first-person tense in your cover letter. The use of the word "I" allows you to discuss your job search situation and accomplishments with a more personal touch.

Be careful, however, as many cover letter writers make the mistake of starting off each sentence with the word "I." It's an easy trap to fall into, since cover letters spend much time relating to your reader things that you have done and achieved. But overuse of the word "I" quickly turns an informational letter into an egotistical letter whose focus is on self rather than the needs of the company. Look to chapter 12 for examples of wording that lets you discuss your accomplishments more eloquently than a long list of "I did ____."

Don't Try for Humor

Since you don't know what pushes your reader's laugh button, when attempting humor in your cover letter you are only tempting fate. Jokes that fall flat are likely to leave a lasting negative impression, and just aren't worth the risk. Save humor for your interview when you can better judge your audience's receptiveness to a light-hearted tone.

GRAMMAR

Keep a watchful eye for misused words and other grammatical errors in your cover letter. Mistakes in grammar make a negative impression that can't be easily undone by even the most alluring exposition of job experience and accomplishments. Your credibility suffers on several fronts, as the hiring manager begins to wonder if you meet even the most basic standards. Subconsciously, he may ask himself:

- Can this job applicant write coherent and grammatically correct business correspondence?
- Can he conduct himself professionally, and make presentations to groups?
- If this applicant doesn't know the difference between "you're" and "your," how observant can she be? Is she oblivious to the details?

The following brief grammatical lessons refer to some of the most common errors found in cover letters.

Phrases to Phase Out

Tired, worn-out clichés elicit a yawn from most employment managers, especially those exposed to cover letter colloquialisms on a regular basis. Even the best cover letters can get torpedoed if they use stale business language that irritates the reader. Try not to sound like everyone else. Avoid trite phrases like "be that as it may," "after all is said and done," "few and far between," and "should this meet with your approval."

You must also avoid sloppy phrases that are considered incorrect on the written page even though they may have become commonplace in spoken language. Phrases such as, "Let's do lunch" or "I'll hook up with you later in the week" are inappropriate for a cover letter.

Study the following common cover letter errors:

In terms of . . .	Try not to overuse this phrase. Rewrite your sentence to be more succinct: "The job appeals to me in terms of responsibilities" could be better stated, "The responsibilities of the job appeal to me."

The foreseeable future   This phrase has become a cliché. Avoid it.

Thank you in advance   This phrase can be construed to mean, "I'll thank you now so I don't have to bother thanking you later." It also sounds a bit presumptuous. Just say thank you, and leave off the "in advance."

 Just because you've seen these phrases on a lot of cover letters doesn't mean you should use them yourself. In fact, it probably means just the opposite!

Needless to say   Exactly. Don't say it.

As you know   This is an unsettling phrase for the reader. Can it be softened to "as you may know"? Can it be left out entirely?

Significant   *Significant* is an adjective that is subjective: One person's "significant" is another person's "*in*significant," so it tells the reader nothing. Same goes for words like *important* and *notable*.

 Heavy use of empty phrases gives the appearance of a blowhard who is trying to cover a serious shortcoming by using overblown language.

Misused and Unnecessary Words

Too many cover letters are full of meaningless or bloated words that do nothing to promote your case for getting hired, and instead take up space and dilute the strength of your message. And still other letters are full of words that are used incorrectly. Watch for these pitfalls:

Up	The word *up* is frequently joined with such words as *head, start, add,* and *think.* These words are more powerful if you don't dilute them with the word *up* at the end. Thus, you *head* rather than *head up* a project, and *add the figures* rather than *add up the figures.*
Out	Same as *up.* Tends to be added to words such as *try, check,* and *watch.*

As you write your letter, consider whether the phrase you are using adds anything to the meaning of the sentence. If not, it is unnecessary and is better left out.

Off	Same again. You *start* rather than *start off.*
Utilize	Getting hackneyed; sounds like resume-ese. How 'bout plain old *use*?

Whenever you have the option to use a big word or a simple word, choose the simple word. It adds charm and credibility to your letter.

Fact	Be careful not to overuse this word when referring to matters of judgment. Everything that you call a fact should be capable of concrete verification.
Heighth	*Heighth* is not a word, but a popular mispronunciation of the word *height.*
Anxious	Connotes anxiety and apprehension. Better to use the word *eager,* as in "I am eager to hear from you."

Orientated	*Orientated* isn't correct English. Use *oriented*.
Hopefully	Although it has come into popular use, using *hopefully* to mean "I hope" (as in "Hopefully, I will hear from you next week"*)* is wrong. Whether used correctly or not, the word weakens your look of confidence. Avoid it in your cover letter.
Myself	Many speakers and writers incorrectly use this as a formal version of *me,* as in "Carl asked Lorrie and myself to join the team." The word *me* is correct; *myself* is not.
Yourself	*Yourself* is not a substitute for *you.* It is fine to say, "I plan to call Mr. Peters and you early next week." It is wrong to say, "I plan to call Mr. Peters and yourself early next week."
	(The best phrasing puts the reader first: "I plan to call you and Mr. Peters early next week.")
Be sure and	Should be *be sure to,* as in "I'll be sure to contact Bill on Tuesday."
Try and	Write *try to* rather than *try and*: "I will try to reach Bob Simons on Thursday."
Wait on	Write *wait for* rather than *wait on,* unless you are applying for a job as a waiter serving tables.

The Context

Some words appear on cover letters in the wrong context. Not only can this be confusing for your reader, it can be deadly to your chances of getting a job offer. Some differences can be subtle, so beware.

Your, you're	Watch your grammar here! Pay attention to the difference: *You're* is a contraction of *you* and *are,* while *your* shows ownership: "You're known as a decisive manager" and "Your co-worker suggested I contact you."
Learn, teach	*Learn* means to acquire knowledge; *teach* means to give out knowledge. Thus, you *teach* a class, where the students *learn* facts.
Accept, except	*Accept* means to receive; *except* means to leave out. Thus, "I accepted a position at ABC Company" and "I oversaw all aspects of the new product line except production scheduling."
Effect, affect	*Effect* as a noun means result. As a verb, it means to bring about or to accomplish. Don't confuse this with *affect,* which means to influence. For example, "Bonuses can affect an employee's behavior" and "The new marketing strategy effected astonishing results."
Farther, further	There is a difference in the usage of these two words. *Farther* should be used to denote distance; *further* connotes time or quantity. Thus, you drive *farther*; you pursue a sales lead *further.*
Regard, regards	*Regard* can be used to mean reference ("In regard to our meeting . . . "). *Regards,* on the other hand, means greetings. It is thus incorrect to say, "With regards to your letter . . . " However, it is correct to say "as regards," which means "In regard to . . . " as in "As regards our conversation . . . "

Less, fewer	*Fewer* means "a smaller number." *Less* means "not so much." Use *fewer* whenever you refer to something that can be counted; for example, "fewer calories" and "less time."
Criterion, criteria	A *criterion* is a standard test by which something is measured or compared. Criterion is the singular form. *Criteria,* the plural form, is often incorrectly used as the singular.
Assure, ensure, insure	Pay attention here: To *assure* is to state that something will be or has been accomplished. To *ensure* is to make certain of something. Leave the word *insure* to the insurance companies.
Regime, regimen	*Regimen* means routine, while *regime* means rule. Thus, you can have a steady *regimen* of tight deadlines, but not a *regime* of deadlines.
There, their, they're	Back to grammar school for these commonly misused words. *There* denotes location. *Their* shows ownership, as in "their year-end report." *They're* is the contraction for "they are," as in "They're interested in meeting me this week."

EDITING THE FINAL PRODUCT

Don't beat yourself up if your cover letter isn't perfect on the first try. A first draft is just that—a draft—a mere outline or sketch meant to be reworked and reformulated until it says what you want it to say.

Although your final letter should only be one page in length, you shouldn't necessarily start out trying for one page. If you do, you may end up with only a couple of terse, flimsy sentences. Start out writing everything important that you can think of. It will then take some skillful whittling to get your letter to the optimal one-page length, but at least you won't have forgotten to include any of the important details. If the letter turns out to be too long, cut ruthlessly to get it down to the one-page length.

 As you begin to write, your concentration should not be on the length of your letter, but on its contents.

After you've created your letter as you envisioned it, look it over from the perspective of a tired hiring manager. Ask yourself if the letter:

- Opens with an attention-getter?
- Is too long? (one-page limit!)
- Is trite? If they've heard it a hundred times before, it won't impress them.
- Addresses the company's needs as I understand them?
- Emphasizes my strongest skills?
- Uses action verbs to describe my accomplishments and skills?
- Includes my telephone number and e-mail address, if appropriate?
- Takes the initiative for follow up?

CHAPTER SUMMARY

In this chapter, you learned to use style, tone, and grammar effectively in your cover letter, and you learned to edit your draft into a well-polished final product.

CHAPTER 12

Cover Letter Templates

In this chapter, you are given templates to refer to when writing your cover letters. These can help you with the layout and phrasing of your letters, as you plug your own information into pre-written sentences.

Often, the hardest part of writing the cover letter is not deciding which facts to include, but how and where to include them. Fitting the facts in with just the right amount of explanation is tricky.

This chapter helps ease your writing pains by offering multiple wording options for each piece of your cover letter. Plug your individual information into one of the prepared templates to develop a customized cover letter that effectively conveys your knowledge and skills. By using the templates in this chapter, you'll save time and alleviate stress, leaving you more time and energy for important things like company research and networking.

MAKING TEMPLATES WORK FOR YOU

This chapter contains templates that you can use to craft traditional letters to companies of interest, letters in response to an ad, or letters to a recruiting firm. You are offered a sampling of paragraphs with different phrasings, so that you can plug in particular elements of your background as you need.

Using templates is effective only if you work diligently to make each letter specific to a particular company or job opportunity. Each letter should focus on the things that are important to each case, so don't let yourself get lazy and plug in facts without examining what the needs of the organization might be.

The key to using these templates successfully is to consider them to be pieces of a puzzle. Turn them around, line them up, reorganize them to meet your needs, and see how they fit into the big picture. Feel free to use any of these paragraphs as they are, or snip bits and pieces from several paragraphs to create your own masterpiece. As you rework them, ask yourself these questions:

- Does my letter focus on the key issues that will interest the organization I am addressing?
- Have I covered everything I had hoped to?
- Is the letter easy to read ?
- Does it flow logically from one point to the next?
- Does it sound canned?
- Will it make me stand out from other job applicants?

As you read the sample paragraphs, try to plug your own information into the areas in brackets. These have been filled in with fictitious facts to give you a feel for how the sentences should sound, but obviously the words in parentheses must be replaced by your own words in order for the sentence to work.

Don't get thrown off by the words in brackets. While those job titles and career fields may have nothing to do with yours, the general phrasing of the sentences may be just the thing to fit your cover letter needs.

TRADITIONAL LETTER TEMPLATES

Opening Phrases

Examples:

My research indicates that your firm has been moving decisively into the [environmental services] industry. Perhaps my background in [environmental engineering] might be of some use to you as your emphasis shifts toward this direction.

In just 10 weeks, I will be moving to [Chicago] and am bringing with me [six] solid years of [financial management] experience. I'd like to put this experience to work for your company.

An employee of your company, [Nancy Wimmer], told me that you could use strong [computer skills] in your office. In my last six years as [office manager] of [Shore Conn, Inc.], I worked with computers in many capacities, such as:

- Job example #1
- Job example #2
- Job example #3

[Lee Wheeler], a project coordinator with your company, tells me that there is a great team spirit at [Temple Communications]. She said the people who work there take pride in their work, and strive hard to uphold the company's fine reputation. As a recent college graduate with a degree in [graphic design], your company is the place I want to be.

I have been reading the recent articles in the [*Butler Chronicle*] about your company's relocation to [Fairfield]. As you make this transition, perhaps you will be in need of people with experience in [customer service].

Are you in search of an experienced [health services specialist], with knowledge of [skill #1], [skill #2], and [skill #3]? I have [seven] years of solid experience in these areas with particular expertise in:

- Skill #4
- Skill #5
- Skill #6

Options for the Letter Body

Examples:

My experience at [Colson Manufacturing] has given me the opportunity to learn a broad range of skills, including [skill #1], [skill #2], and [skill #3]. My recent accomplishments as [operations specialist] are:

- Accomplishment #1
- Accomplishment #2
- Accomplishment #3

Over the last [10 years], I have gained valuable knowledge in many aspects of the [mortgage banking industry]. Recently, I [accomplishment]. I was also able to [accomplishment].

I have had extensive experience in the [facilities management] industry, including the last [four years] as [project manager] at [Lowe and O'Brien, Inc.]. My work in [project and facilities management] has taught me [personal skill], and given me first-hand experience in [skill area] and [skill area].

As a recent college graduate, my experience in the work world is limited. But as a straight-A student at [Miami University], I learned valuable skills such as [skill #1] and [skill #2], which I will take with me to the workplace.

My [12 years] of successful [public relations] experience in well-known, Fortune 100 companies has given me the ability to work well under pressure and to meet the challenge of even the toughest deadlines. My [personal skill #1] and [personal skill #2] have enabled me to succeed where others might fail.

Closing Statements

Examples:

I am confident that I can make a significant contribution to your organization. I will call you later in the week to see if we might discuss potential opportunities at [Spencer Technologies]. Thank you for your consideration.

I will be calling you sometime next week to follow up on this letter. I hope to be able to schedule a personal meeting with you so that I might learn more about your company and its goals.

I would appreciate the opportunity to meet with you personally. I think you would find that I have [personal skill #1] and [personal skill #2], and I would enjoy putting them to work for [Perman Associates]. I will call you early next week to see if we might find a convenient meeting time.

Attached is my resume, which outlines some of my other qualifications. I would enjoy meeting with you to discuss them personally. I will call you later in the week to follow up. Thanks for your time.

I hope to replicate these results in your organization. I will call you on Thursday or Friday to talk with you as a follow-up to this letter. Your time and consideration are much appreciated.

AD RESPONSE LETTER TEMPLATES

Opening Phrases

Examples:

Your advertisement in the [*San Francisco Chronicle*] has caught my interest. I have a strong background in [personnel administration], which directly relates to the position you advertised.

I am responding to your advertisement in [*The Cincinnati Enquirer*] on [date]. As you can see, the skills I have achieved in my [12 years] as [sales manager] for [Procter and Gamble] directly relate to the position you have available.

Your ad captured my attention. My skills are a perfect match to the requirements you listed in the [*Washington Post*].

I recently read your ad in the [*Baltimore Sun*] for a position as a [youth services director]. My candidacy for this position is advanced by my experience in three areas: [elementary education certification], [a master's degree in counseling], and [three years' experience at a youth home for boys].

The skills you require for the position of [CAD engineer] match my skills and background exactly.

In reading your advertisement in the [*Boston Globe*] on [date], I noticed that the skills you require seem to match my professional strengths.

My professional background matches the skills you are seeking.

My strengths and your needs are a perfect match.

I read with great interest your advertisement in the [*Mason Pulse*] on [date].

Your advertisement in the [date] issue of the [*New York Times*] piqued my interest. Please allow me to highlight my background as it relates to your requirements.

Options for the Body

Examples:

Your ad states that you are looking for [skill #1], [skill #2], and [skill #3]. Let me tell you how my background matches those skills directly:

- Example of skill #1 from current or recent work situation
- Example of skill #2 from current or recent work situation
- Example of skill #3 from current or recent work situation

Your ad mentions that you are looking for someone with a strong background in [skill #1]. A recent accomplishment of mine demonstrates that skill:

[Describe your accomplishment in two to three sentences].

I have a great deal of experience with [skill or industry mentioned in ad] at [company name], which has given me a firm foundation in [skill #1] and [skill #2].

I believe that I am particularly well-qualified for your position based on the following examples of my recent accomplishments:

- Accomplishment #1
- Accomplishment #2
- Accomplishment #3

My candidacy for this position is advanced by my qualifications in three areas mentioned in the ad: [skill #1], [skill #2], and [skill #3]. My experience in these areas includes:

- Example of related work or accomplishment
- Example of related work or accomplishment
- Example of related work or accomplishment

You mentioned that the ideal candidate would possess [# years of experience]. I have [three years of experience]. Your ad also mentions [skill #1]. I have an extensive background in all aspect of [skill #1], including [specifics of skill #1]. I also have strong experience in [skill #2], most notably [details of skill #2].

Closing Statements

Examples:

I would like to tell you more about my background, and would appreciate a meeting with you at your convenience. I will call you later in the week to see if we might find a time to talk, or you can reach me at [phone #]. Thanks for your time.

I am available to meet with you to discuss your needs and my skills at your convenience. You can reach me at [phone #] or by e-mail at [e-mail address]. Thank you for your consideration.

I have other areas of expertise that may be of interest to you. I will call you later in the week to see if we might set up a time to discuss them in person. Or, you can reach me at [phone #]. Thank you for your time.

I will call you early next week to see if we might arrange a time to meet. If you'd like to reach me, you can call me at my office at [phone #], or at my home, [phone #]. Thank you for your consideration.

I will call you later this week to discern your interest in my qualifications. Or, you can reach me at [phone #] or by e-mail at [e-mail address] to set up a meeting. Thank you for your time, and I look forward to talking with you soon.

I will call you over the next several days to set up an appointment. If you prefer, you can reach me at [phone #], or leave a message at [pager]. Thank you for your time.

I will contact you in a few days to discuss my qualifications in further detail. You can also reach me at [phone #]. Thanks, and I look forward to talking with you soon.

I look forward to discussing my skills and your needs in more detail. I will call you later in the week to see if we might find a time to meet. If you would like to reach me, my number is [phone #]. Thanks for your time.

I look forward to the possibility of meeting with you to discuss the position in more detail. I will call you within the next several days to find a time that is convenient. Thanks for your consideration.

Feel free to contact me at [phone #] if you have any questions. I will contact you toward the end of the week to see if we might schedule a personal interview. Thank you for your time. I look forward to talking with you soon.

RECRUITER LETTER TEMPLATES

Opening Phrases

Examples:

Please consider my name if you are conducting a search for an [MIS professional].

I understand that you are frequently asked to locate [senior marketing executives] with strong abilities in market analysis and profitability.

A former client of yours, [Ellen Dillon] with [BFI, Inc.], suggested I contact you because of your expertise in industries involving [unionized manufacturing environments].

As you conduct your search assignments, you may need a [sales management professional]. I have over [11 years] of successful experience in [route sales], and have enjoyed a progressive career in management of other sales personnel.

My eight years of progressive success in [brand management] may be of interest to you and your clients.

Perhaps one of your current or future clients will have an interest in my [senior level operations management] experience.

It has come to my attention that your firm specializes in placing [human resources professionals]. I have five years of mid-level experience in [HR] at [ABC Company] and am sending my resume to your attention.

Do any of your current search assignments call for a [senior-level purchasing professional]? If so, my credentials may be of interest to you.

I understand that your organization deals extensively with placing [administrative professionals]. I have six progressive years as an [administrative secretary] with [ABC Company], and three successful years as an [office manager] with [Kemper Inc.].

Options for the Letter Body

Examples:

I have [six years'] experience in [desktop publishing], with expertise in [skill area]. The following are highlights of my track record:

- Accomplishment #1
- Accomplishment #2
- Accomplishment #3

My broad background in the [health services] industry includes [three years] as a [billing specialist]. In this capacity, I learned the importance of a solid foundation in [skill #1] and [skill #2]. My accomplishments include:

- Accomplishment #1
- Accomplishment #2
- Accomplishment #3

During my career with such Fortune 500 companies as [company #1] and [company #2], I worked to improve the efficiency of their [department name]. These improvements include:

- Improvement #1
- Improvement #2
- Improvement #3

My experience as an [insurance industry] executive might pique the interest of some of your clients. While with [name of company], I had the opportunity to gain expertise in [skill #1] and [skill #2], as a sample of my accomplishments demonstrate:

- Accomplishment #1
- Accomplishment #2
- Accomplishment #3

Your clients may find my experience in [human resources] particularly compelling when they consider these key accomplishments:

- [year accomplishment was made]: Accomplishment #1
- [year accomplishment was made]: Accomplishment #2
- [year accomplishment was made]: Accomplishment #3

The [number of years] I have spent in [marketing] have made me aware of the importance of [skill #1], [skill #2], and [skill #3]. I was able to hone these skills while working on key projects, such as:

- Project #1
- Project #2
- Project #3

Closing Statements

Examples:

I can be reached at my office on a confidential basis at [phone #].

You can reach me at [phone #], and I have asked my staff to forward your message immediately if I am unavailable when you call. I look forward to an interesting new career opportunity through your firm.

If you don't currently have need of my expertise, please include my name in your job search database for future reference. Thanks for your consideration.

If you are aware of a suitable opportunity with one of your clients, you can reach me any time at [phone #] or at [e-mail address]. Thank you for your consideration.

My current income is in the [$50–$60K] range, and I look forward to a new opportunity in a similar range. I would like to stay in the [Northern Pennsylvania/New York] region, but will consider a broader geographic area. Thank you for keeping me in mind as you work with your client companies.

I appreciate your time as you consider my credentials for your clients' needs. You can reach me at [phone #], or by e-mail at [e-mail address]. I look forward to the possibility of working with you.

I look forward to the possibility of talking with you personally. Please call at your convenience; I'd like to explore potential opportunities more fully. You can reach me at [phone #]. You can also e-mail me at [e-mail address]. Thank you for your time.

CHAPTER SUMMARY

In this chapter, you were given samples of paragraphs to use like pieces of a puzzle to help you put together an outstanding cover letter one section at a time.

CHAPTER 13

Letters of Reference and Recommendation

In this chapter, you will learn to collect a list of references and letters of recommendation that will impress a potential employer.

REFERENCE LISTS

A reference list is a prepared listing of the contact information of colleagues, business associates, and friends who know you well and are willing to give you a glowing recommendation to an inquiring employer.

You may want to include a brief mention of your references in your cover letter, since this notation is no longer a standard part of the resume. Mentioning references is not a required part of the cover letter (most hiring managers will not become concerned with your references until after the interview process), but by mentioning them you imply that you're confident in your abilities and have personal testimonies to back up your success.

Whether you mention it on your cover letter or not, take care to have a carefully prepared list of references ready in case a hiring manager requests that one be sent.

Never include your reference list on your cover letter, or include it with your resume and cover letter package. Let the employer request it before you send it.

Compiling Your List

When writing your list, include three to six names of people who will be willing to speak with a potential employer about your positive personal and professional attributes. Be sure to choose people who know about your accomplishments and who will give you enthusiastic praise!

When considering your references, first write a "long list" of potential candidates. Think of everyone you have recently come in contact with, both professionally and personally, who could vouch for your character and work ethic. Consider colleagues who have made positive comments about your work, or bosses who have been impressed with your performance. Then narrow your candidates to a "short list" according to these criteria:

- **The longer the association, the better.** A reference who has known you for 15 years holds a lot more weight than someone who blurts out that he's only worked with you on a single project.

- **Consider the relationship.** Former bosses and colleagues are more convincing references than personal friends and relatives, because they are less likely to stretch the truth and will know your work habits more intimately.

- **How recent is the contact?** Relationships that dwindled away to nothing 10 years ago aren't strong reference choices, because the reference can't attest to your current work style. Look for people with whom you have interacted recently.

- **Evaluate communication skills.** If your reference can't communicate well over the telephone, it will be hard for her to impress your potential new employer. Choose someone who is articulate, can communicate enthusiasm, and speaks clearly.

Make sure every person you have chosen as a reference knows that he or she is included on your list! If your references are unaware they may be called, they are likely to act hesitant and unsure when answering questions about you. At best, this makes you look like you neglected the details of your job search. At worst, it may make the hiring manager suspicious that you have something to hide, and you may very well lose the job offer because of it.

Eight Keys to Producing an Impressive Reference List

Study the suggestions below before compiling your reference list.

1. Get permission from every person you plan to include on your list before you begin.

2. Be sure to write your name and telephone number at the top of your reference list. If it somehow becomes separated from the other documents in your application dossier, it can be identified as yours.

3. Choose former bosses, co-workers, professional associates, or people of status in the community who can attest to your professional integrity and effectiveness.

4. Your list can include family, friends, or neighbors who are willing to attest to your excellent character, but use no more than two non-business acquaintances on a list of five or more references.

5. List each name with an address, phone number, and job title (or descriptive title).

6. Your list should be neat, error-free, and centered neatly upon the page.

7. It should be typed in a font that matches your resume font.

8. The paper for your reference list should match your resume paper.

Bring several copies of your reference list with you to all interviews. Be sure to offer it to the employer at the end of the interview, if he hasn't already requested it. Don't, however, pull it from your briefcase and hand it to him without first being asked to do so. Simply alert him to the fact that you have brought one with you, and would be happy to let him have one if he'd like to see it.

Sample Reference List

Reference List For

PATTI RESTICK
(410) 555 2916

Dr. Paul Mechstein, President
Summerville and Mechstein, Inc.
12116 Bright Place
Columbia, MD 21044
(410) 555-7869

Shiela Chaker, Lab Director
Siena Biotech
1344 Technology Place
Fort Worth TX 22377
(619) 555-9080

Cleo Lichten, Associate Professor
Biology Department
Northland College
Ashland, WI 55212
(719) 555-3065

Lee Westgate, Owner
Westgate Financial
6 Plaza Center
Columbia, MD 21044
(410) 555-9774

LETTERS OF RECOMMENDATION

Occasionally, you are asked to supply an employer with a letter of recommendation. You may simply wish to request one from a trusted manager or colleague to use throughout your job search. Follow these guidelines as you consider a letter of recommendation:

- When asking someone to write a letter of recommendation, give him or her a specific time when you need the letter to be completed. Try to allow about two weeks for completion. Leaving the completion date open-ended creates the possibility of embarrassment on both sides if the person hasn't written it and you have to ask for it.

- Give the person a copy of your resume or a list of your skills to use when writing the letter. Even if you have worked closely with the person and you think he is already familiar with your skills and accomplishments, he will appreciate having your resume to refresh his memory.

- If you are sending the recommendation letter in response to a specific job opening, give the letter writer a copy of the job listing, if possible. This allows him to tailor the letter to address the employer's needs.

- Write a thank-you note to each person who took the time to compose a letter for you. If they can take the time out of their busy day to do you a favor, it is important for you to show your appreciation. Remember, this person might also be called upon to give you a verbal recommendation!

OTHER LETTERS TO HAVE AVAILABLE

As your job search begins, think of any other written praise you may have received throughout your professional experience. This may include:

- Positive performance reviews
- Letters from bosses or supervisors in praise of a particular project you were associated with
- Thank-you letters from clients for excellent service

See chapter 17 for tips on how to construct these letters.

Do not include these letters with your resume and cover letter. Save them for follow-up correspondence or interview situations.

CHAPTER SUMMARY

In this lesson, you learned to use letters of reference, recommendation, and praise to make a positive impression on potential employers.

CHAPTER 14

Your Job Search Campaign

In this chapter, you will learn to take your job search into your own hands by finding companies that appeal to you and targeting those companies in your job campaign. You will learn tried-and-true techniques and interesting new ideas for conducting a job search that is efficient and focused.

GET OFF TO A GOOD START

You've worked hard to prepare an impressive and polished cover letter that will open the door to many job opportunities. The trick now is knowing where to *find* those opportunities.

Before plunging in to your search, consider these points:

- The key to a successful job search is not how hard you work, but how *smart* you work.

- Job search success is not found in the quantity of resumes you send out, but in the *quality* of the contacts you make.

- You will find success not by letting the winds of fate blow you to and fro. A job search becomes successful when you take control of the sail and steer yourself where you want to go.

- Successful job search strategies aren't for the faint of heart. Wimps and weaklings beware! You must be decisive, take risks, get gutsy, and persevere!

- A rejection doesn't mean you aren't good enough. Sometimes rejection just happens, rightly or wrongly. Remember, the Beatles were rejected by the first record companies they approached!

UNDERSTANDING THE JOB MARKET

The job market consists of potential employers and active job seekers working diligently to find each other. Employers use a variety of tactics to try to locate and hire talented people, and job seekers work equally hard trying to track down employers with good job opportunities.

The job market is in a constant state of flux as new positions open and others close. Job possibilities can open when:

- Employees are promoted.
- Employees are transferred to a new location.
- Employees retire.
- Companies expand.
- New industries emerge.
- Older industries change form.
- Companies merge or reorganize.

 You are not alone! Each year, almost 20 percent of all working people find themselves engaged in a job or career change.

DECIDING WHERE YOU WANT TO WORK

An important part of any job search campaign is narrowing the focus of your efforts. The possibilities for job openings are endless! Even the most staid and stable companies experience at least *some* turnover. Successful, goal-oriented job seekers have a clearly defined plan of action. They target specific companies on which to focus their attention and know what to say to generate interest.

Too many job seekers go about the critical early steps the wrong way. Rather than proactively exploring a variety of companies and focusing on those that are the best fit, many job seekers simply wait to see which companies advertise openings in the local paper, and then apply there. This system of job searching is equivalent to searching for a mate by planting yourself on a stool at the local bar and waiting to see who shows up.

Don't sit passively while the winds of fate buffet you about. Take your job search into your own hands, decide where it is you want to work, and act decisively to get a job there!

STARTING TO EXPLORE

Getting started may be the hardest part of the company exploration process, because corporate connections and job opportunities seem so inaccessible. There isn't one handy single list that tells you the names of all local companies, where they are located, what they make or sell, and what kind of people they hire.

You might be surprised, however, how many resources are available that give you a good solid piece of the research puzzle, and get you started on your way to the job that you desire.

KNOW WHAT YOU'RE LOOKING FOR

Before you begin your exploration, take some time to think about your needs and goals in order to narrow the field a bit. Consider your options according to these criteria:

- **Your interests**   Examine what kind of work you find enjoyable. What sorts of responsibilities are energizing to you? What makes you feel successful? What skills and experience do you have?

- **Geography**   Where do you want to work? Do you want to stay where you are now, or do you have plans to move to a different part of the country or the world?

- **Commute**   How much time do you want to spend each morning and evening on the road? What is your absolute limit? Be realistic, because what may sound bearable now may become absolutely unbearable day after day after day.

- **Corporate culture**   What kind of atmosphere do you prefer? If you are planning to stay with your new job for the long term, it needs to be a place where you feel like a part of it. Do you want a comfortable, laid-back environment, or a hard-driving, get-ahead atmosphere?

- **Devotion to your career**   Do you mind working in a place that requires you to put in a lot of hours to get ahead? Are you willing to travel or work weekends as needed? Think about your needs in terms of personal or family time versus work time.

- **Your future**   Will the company be a good place for you to be over the long term? Are there opportunities for advancement in your field? Will you be learning new things and advancing your skills?

- **Size of the company**   What kind of company appeals to you: a corporate Goliath, a tiny start-up, or something in between?

Once you've answered these questions for yourself, then you've begun the focusing process that will help you center your search on the companies that appeal to you most.

> Don't pay any attention to which companies are hiring or who has the job openings. All you want to do at this stage is find the companies that are most appealing to you.

THE RESEARCH

Now that you know what kind of company you are looking for, it's time to begin your research to find out if such companies exist. There are plenty of places to look!

The Library

Maybe the easiest and least intimidating place to start your research is the local library. There you will find amazing reference books that answer just about any question you might ever think of asking about any company. Start off with these basics:

- *Dun & Bradstreet*
- *Standard & Poor's*
- *Moody's Million Dollar Directory*
- *Value Line Investments*

Don't miss the other reference books that are specific to particular fields. You should find informative books on health organizations, technology companies, manufacturing firms, and many more. Ask the reference librarian for help if you can't find the books you need.

While you are in the library, be sure to ask the reference librarian if they have a database of companies. Many libraries have national, state, or local databases of corporations that are designed for job seekers. These often include loads of company information, along with contact names of department heads, and allow you to conduct searches for companies that meet your criteria.

Your Local Newspaper's Business Pages

Make it a daily ritual to scan the local business pages for news about area organizations. You're likely to find information on key personnel changes, mergers, relocations, expansions, and other tidbits that can help you discover opportunities that other job seekers may not be aware of. If you don't currently subscribe to the daily paper, make the investment today. For a small price you'll reap substantial rewards.

The Chamber of Commerce

Your local chamber of commerce is likely to have a list of area businesses that may include addresses, telephone numbers, and names of potential contacts. If they don't have the kind of list you are looking for, ask them where else you might check.

To reach your local chamber of commerce online, try typing in the name of your state and then "chamber of commerce." This should lead you to a directory of local chapters.

The Local Economic Development Office

Don't overlook the city or county office of economic development or planning office. These are the folks who work to attract new businesses to the local area, and are often the first to know when a new organization is set to arrive. Give them a call and briefly describe your skills and experience. Ask for the phone numbers of companies that are slated to begin operations in the area.

Professional Associations

In today's business climate, professional associations abound, and they can be extremely helpful in making connections with people in your field of interest. To find local chapters of professional associations, try looking in *The Encyclopedia of Associations,* which you can find at the local library. Or try playing around on the Internet. You can search under "professional associations" and hone in on specifics from there, or start with a narrower focus, such as "engineering professional associations."

The Internet

The Internet is a good source for finding companies by geographic region and field of specialty. Try searching by the name of your city plus "companies," or try something like "Ohio manufacturing companies" or "Pennsylvania technology companies." To get to the subcategories, go to "business and companies."

Look up each company's Web site and snoop around for tidbits of history, company news, financial information, and recent events. Many Web sites, by the way, list current job openings at their firm.

It is certainly advisable to apply to any openings that interest you, but don't concentrate your energy on the positions that are listed as open. Instead, focus your energy on establishing contact with the people with the power to make decisions about hiring you at the company you like in the department that fits you best.

Business and Trade Magazines

Search business and trade magazines for interesting articles on growing companies. Reference librarians are usually very helpful in tracking down particular articles. You might also try searching for articles on the Internet. Larger corporations in particular tend to yield amazing online results. Try typing in the name of the company and the word "articles" and then click Search. IBM and Microsoft, for example, list many interesting articles and provide links to many more.

> Pay attention to the names of the people who authored or were quoted in the articles you find in business and trade magazines. Try sending a cover letter and resume directly to their attention, and enclose a copy of the article with your letter!

As you explore specific news on each company, examine the information with an eye for things you might include in the first line of your attention-grabbing cover letter: recent acquisitions, company expansion, relocation, growth in certain aspects, and so on. Your knowledge of what is happening with the company will help throughout your job search campaign.

Friends in the Business

Nobody has better information about local companies than people who work for rival companies in the same geographic area. If you know someone who might have access to the information you need, ask! You might find that your friend has lists of local firms with contact names, or even a personal contact so you can begin to network.

More than 70 percent of new jobs are found through personal contacts and referrals. Don't focus only on business colleagues. Everyone you have a conversation with is a potential job contact.

WHAT NEXT?

As you unearth companies that appeal to you, be careful to write down the pertinent information that will help you in your job search. You might even want to make several copies of a template sheet to fill in for each company you find. Leave spaces for the following information:

- Company name
- Company address
- Web address
- Name of CEO or president
- Departmental guide (a breakdown of corporate departments)
- Contact name (head of the department in which you'd like to work)
- Contact phone number
- Number of employees
- Brief history and overview of company

THE BATTLE PLAN

Now what? You've worked hard at the research and unearthed a long, luscious list of companies that are ripe for your resume and cover letter. But do you really have to send cover letters to *all* those companies? The answer is yes—but happily, not all at once.

Comb your list for the crème de la crème: those 10 or so companies that stand above the others as absolute top priorities. These will be the first potential employers to receive your letter and resume.

Several days following your first mailing, send off your package to the next 10 or so companies on the list. Why not send out as many as you can all at once, you ask? Because in each and every one of those cover letters, you promised to follow up your correspondence with a telephone call. If you send out 300 letters in a day, that's 300 telephone calls you are going to have to make, as you said in your letter, "early next week." Spacing out your mailings has the benefit of spacing out your follow-up calls.

Continue to add to this top priority list as your search progresses. Don't make the mistake of thinking that your company research work is over and done. Your job search campaign must be a progressive project. It's like pushing a big boulder across the ground. If you get the momentum going, the rock becomes quite easy to move. But let it stop, and it takes a great exertion of energy to get it going again.

 The key to your strategy is to send out a volume of letters that is heavy enough to keep the action going, yet realistic enough to allow you to make your follow-up calls.

COORDINATE YOUR CAMPAIGN

Don't concentrate all your energy in one place. There are other aspects of your job search that you mustn't neglect. Review this checklist of job search strategies daily:

- **Have you contacted any local employment agencies or search firms today?** Are there any in the area who have not heard from you yet? Are there any agencies you've contacted with whom you've let the conversation lag? Don't let your contacts with recruiting firms and employment agencies run dry!

- **Are you checking your sources for job advertisements on a daily basis?** Job ads are everywhere: in the newspaper, in trade magazines, on the Internet, on bulletin boards. Keep up the steady pace of advertisement responses, and you'll reap the benefits when the interviews roll in.

- **Are you keeping the lines of networking communications buzzing?** Are you contacting acquaintances and colleagues to alert them to your job search? Are you talking with fellow association members and others who are connected in your field?

Don't let job interviews slow you down. Many job seekers slacken their efforts when the interviews begin, figuring that a job offer will quickly come through. If it doesn't, however, all that effort is wasted. Many a job campaign has been derailed this way.

BALANCE YOUR EFFORTS

It is vital that you coordinate your cover letter mailings so that you are stirring up business in several pots at once. In any one day, send some of your letters to recruiting agencies, some to advertised job openings, some to networking contacts, and some to targeted companies. With all those pots churning around, something is bound to boil.

Where does all this lead you? Most assuredly, not only to finding a job more quickly, but also to a better job. After all, if you steadily prod potential employment markets, you will most likely turn up multiple opportunities and multiple job offers. How does it sound to be able to choose your favorite from among the many job offers? Worth the work? Absolutely.

CHAPTER SUMMARY

In this chapter, you learned to take a proactive approach to your job search by discovering which companies you'd like to work for, learning more about them, and sending your cover letter and resume there.

CHAPTER 15

Using the Web in Your Job Search

In this lesson, you will learn about job searching and posting resumes on the Web. You will also learn about e-mailing resumes and cover letters.

ONLINE JOB SEARCH BASICS

The art of conducting a job search hasn't been the same since the Internet came into popular use. No longer is a job search limited to who you know or what you can read in the classified job ads. The Web abounds with opportunities to connect with other job seekers and with employers, to explore career possibilities across the globe, and to research opportunities and companies that interest you.

To begin your online adventure, try using the keywords "job" or "career" to search the Web. This will give you a broad picture of what job search choices the Web has in store for you. The following list merely scratches the surface of the possibilities available to you:

- You can peruse the booths at virtual job fairs in any location, and forward your resume and cover letter to the companies there.

- You can use a personal job shopper service which will browse a database of jobs for you, then automatically e-mail any matches to your address.

- You can post a homepage resume and cover letter that goes online and allows you to receive e-mail or an instant message from other job seekers or potential employers.

- You can ask advice of career experts about your own particular career issues.

- You can even add video to your online resume so that prospective employers can see and hear you talking about your career credentials.

 The possibilities are exciting and the opportunities great, but don't get so caught up in using the Web that you neglect your other job search methods!

ONLINE RESUME SERVICES

Online resume services are typically full of useful information for anyone searching for a job or just beginning the career exploration process. They usually provide company profiles, recent articles, and job search tips as well as information on writing resumes and cover letters.

Most online services allow you to post your resume free of charge, and give you a password to allow you private access to a list of job openings. Some ask that you use their specific online resume form, which is entered into a searchable database that employers can access for a fee. Do some browsing through a few resume sites to get a feel for how the game is played.

To Post or Not to Post?

Consider these things when deciding whether to post your resume online:

- Would the employers you hope to attract be likely to search the database you are using to post your resume?

- Will your resume and cover letter remain confidential on this system?

- Will this service showcase your resume exclusively?

- Does this database allow your resume to shine, or is there a better way to get a particular employer's attention?

- Does the database to which you're submitting your resume post the types of jobs you are interested in and qualified for?
- How long will your resume stay on this system?
- Once your resume is listed, can it be updated at no cost?
- Will your resume be removed from the database after a certain period of time?

> The posting process is not always confidential. On many sites, you have no control over who can see your resume. Consider this as you contemplate posting.

Company Web Sites

Hiring managers and recruiters are finding the Web to be a quick and inexpensive source for employment advertising that is available to potential candidates 24 hours a day. More and more companies are relying on their own Web site to post jobs and attract job applicants.

You will find that most large American corporations and organizations have their own Web sites, and a good percentage of them post current job openings there. Many allow you to submit a resume electronically in response to a particular opening.

Using company Web sites forces you to do a little career focus work up front, however. If you allow yourself to wander aimlessly through a company's Web pages, you can quickly become distracted and overwhelmed by the vast array of choices. Know what you'd like to do and who you'd like to do it for *before* browsing corporate sites!

E-MAILING YOUR RESUME AND COVER LETTER

Many companies today prefer to receive resumes via e-mail. Successful job seekers prepare a plain text resume that can be sent by e-mail in addition to a hard copy resume that has all the bells and whistles. This plain text document can be sent through e-mail to company sites or cut-and-pasted into forms at online posting sites.

Tips for E-Mailing Resumes and Cover Letters

Before e-mailing your resume and cover letter, consider the following tips:

* Always include a cover letter with your resume. The idea is the same as for hard copies: A cover letter works to enhance your resume by highlighting your strengths and giving it a more personal feel. Send the cover letter in the same e-mail message as your resume.

* If you are e-mailing your resume and cover letter in response to a job ad, fill in the job title or job number in the Subject box.

* Some sites seem ripe with many promising jobs. If you find a site that has continuing promise, you may wish to register your resume at the site. Then you can often simply e-mail a reference number or message to apply for a position in the database.

* Plain-text documents don't use bold, highlights, or underlining. Try using these substitutes to give your plain text some character:

    Use asterisks (*) instead of bullets to make certain lines of text stand out.

    A series of dashes may be used to highlight words or separate sections of your resume.

    Since bold text is not acceptable, try using capital letters to highlight certain words or titles.

THE TOP ONLINE JOB SITES

Several hot sites dominate the myriad Web career sites currently available. No job seeker can do a thorough exploration of today's career possibilities without checking into at least one of these amazing sites. Here are four of them to explore:

1. **www.careermosaic.com**   An extensive site that covers all the angles of the job search, including online job fairs, company Web sites, job postings, and a free resume posting service. Note that they do charge a fee to potential employers who wish to view candidate's resumes.

2. **www.monster.com**   An excellent place to search job postings, research companies, chat with other job seekers, or read up on the latest career happenings. You can even have your resume and cover letter reviewed and critiqued by a professional. Lists nearly 250,000 job opportunities.

3. **www.jobbankusa.com**   Provides employment and resume information services to job candidates, employers, and recruitment firms. Free resume posting service.

4. **www.careerpath.com**   A Web page put together by the newspaper affiliates that offers everything from chat rooms and recent career articles to a resume posting service.

Other Resume and Job Search Hot Spots

Also try these impressive job sites:

www.careermart.com

www.careerbuilder.com

www.ajb.dni.us.com (America's Job Bank)

www.joboptions.com

www.careerweb.com

www.headhunter.net

www.careerShop.com

www.getajob.com

Specialized Job Sites

The following sites cater to the needs of particular categories of job seekers.

Experienced Professionals

www.topjobsusa.com

www.hotjobs.com

Federal Jobs

www.usajobs.opm.gov

www.federaljobs.net

www.fedjobs.com

Students/Recent Graduates

www.jobdirect.com

www.jobtrak.com

Equal Employment Opportunity

www.black-collegian.com

IT/Technical Jobs

www.careermarthi-tech.com

www.topjobsusa.com

Temporary Jobs

www.net-temps.com

Healthcare

www.healthcareerweb.com

Military

www.corporategrayonline.com

There are many more job and resume sites on the Web. The possibilities are endless! Take the time to explore a little and watch the electronic world of job searching unfold before you!

CHAPTER SUMMARY

In this lesson, you learned about online resume services, and explored the job search possibilities that the Web provides.

CHAPTER 16

Following Up After Your Cover Letter Is Sent

*In this chapter, you will learn the most effective
follow-up techniques to use after you send your
cover letter and resume.*

Probably one of the least favorite aspects of the job search campaign is the
follow-up phone call you've promised to make to most of your targeted
companies. Many of the letters you've sent have stated that you will be
calling the company to follow up. An easy thing to say, but not always an
easy thing to do.

Most job seekers have experienced the frustration of making the follow-up
phone call only to find themselves blocked from talking to the hiring manager by a gatekeeping secretary. And even if they do manage to speak to
the employer directly, they often end up feeling awkward or ineffective.

Follow-up phone calls don't have to be failures. In fact, when properly
done, follow-up calls have a high potential to move you forward toward
your job search goal. They offer you the chance to put a voice and personality with the words in your cover letter and resume, placing you far above
the crowd of other job seekers.

WHY FOLLOW-UP CALLS WORK

Here are a few reasons why follow-up phone calls work:

- If you are bold enough to pick up the phone and talk to the employer, you will stand apart in the hiring manager's memory as the professional who was gutsy enough to make the phone call.

- Follow-up calls give you the rare opportunity to sell yourself to the hiring manager in a personal conversation.

- Phone calls give you a chance to discern the needs of the organization more thoroughly than the other job applicants.

- Your phone call proves to the employer that you are a person of integrity: You did exactly what you promised you'd do in your cover letter.

- A personal conversation makes the hiring manager feel she knows you a little better than she knows the rest of the applicants. If she likes what she's heard, you have a sizable jump ahead of the "paper" applicants.

- Hearing your voice allows the hiring manager to get a better feel for your personality. It adds credibility to the claims you've made on your cover letter and resume.

- Making the phone call demonstrates that you are enthusiastic about working for the company.

Follow-up phone calls are valuable only if carried out effectively. How can you ensure that your follow-up calls work for you to maximum effect?

THE TOP EIGHT RULES FOR FRUITFUL FOLLOW-UPS

Before picking up the phone, study the following guidelines.

1. **Don't be vague: Explain your reason for calling at the beginning of the conversation.** If you are calling regarding an open, advertised position, let the employer know up front that this is the reason for your call. Express interest in the position and ask educated questions about the company and the available job. Do not, however, let

yourself be drawn into an on-the-spot telephone interview. These types of interviews tend to be used to weed out job candidates, and are notorious for knocking applicants out of the running.

If you are calling a target company that has not advertised an opening, one effective way to foster a meaningful conversation is to treat the phone call more like a networking experience rather than a job search. Let the employer know that you are in the job market (after all, you've sent your resume), but do not emphasize that you are seeking a job from *him*. Explain that you are doing a bit of "career exploration" before settling into your next position, and trying to meet new people in the industry to learn more and establish new contacts.

2. **Don't ask about the status of your resume. This is a dead-end question.** Calling a hiring manager and asking about your status is a conversation-killer. You will get a pat reply that essentially tells you nothing, and you'll have done nothing to propel your job search forward.

3. **If you are calling regarding a specific job opening, ask what the next step in the hiring process will be.** This question may yield information regarding the time frame of the application process and will let you know when to expect the interviews to take place. This way, you will be keyed in to the most effective times to make other follow-up calls, and make sure that the interviewing process doesn't pass you by. Nothing is more frustrating than wondering what a potential employer is up to, then to finally call and find out that the job you desired has already been filled.

4. **Express interest in a personal meeting.** Let the employer know that you'd like to meet. Whether you call it a formal job interview or merely a chance to chat about the industry and trade contact names, a face-to-face meeting with a decision-maker in the hiring process solidifies your connections much more thoroughly than a phone call can.

5. **Steer the conversation toward the company's needs rather than your own.** Ask educated questions to reflect your interest in the state of their business. Be a good listener. Don't try to cram every pause in the conversation with remarks to glorify your impressive track record.

6. **Use the research you've done to show off your knowledge of the company.** Don't let all that good work you've done go to waste. Any hiring manager at any level will be impressed with a job candidate who's done the homework.

7. **Express your interest in joining the company.** Everybody likes to hear positive things about themselves and the places they are associated with. Tell the employer that you have admired the company or that you are impressed with its solid reputation. Listen carefully to insider remarks, and respond with positive comments and praise.

8. **Call the person to whom you wrote the letter, not personnel.** Probably the most important rule for effective follow-up calls is to talk to the person with the power to hire. Conversing with the human resources folks is akin to standing at the gatehouse in front of the manor and chatting with the gatekeeper. HR professionals are there to act as liaison between you and the hiring manager; they are not usually the decision-makers in the hiring process. Don't concentrate your energy on the middleman! Go directly to the source.

GETTING PAST THE GATEKEEPER

It isn't always easy to reach the hiring manager. Many have receptionists who consider it their duty to keep such phone calls from disrupting the day of the managers they work for.

With this in mind, it isn't wise to tell the hiring manager's secretary that you are a job seeker unless you are responding to a particular advertised job opening. Many administrative people might not understand the networking nature of your call, and will assume that you should discuss your job interests with the personnel department.

It isn't wise to fib about your reason for calling, either. If you say that your phone call is personal, for example, many hiring managers will feel that you tricked them into picking up the phone, which isn't likely to engender cordial feelings toward you.

So how do you persuade the receptionist to put you through to the hiring manager? Try being honest, but perhaps a bit vague, as in:

Receptionist: What is the reason for your call?

You: This is a follow-up to some correspondence. She should be expecting my call.

or:

You: Ms. Smith is aware that I'll be calling. I've contacted her regarding a business situation of mine.

or:

You: I have some quick questions regarding your recent merger.

or:

You: I'm looking for some information on your relocation to Glencoe.

or:

You: I have some questions about an article I read on your company.

or:

You: I was hoping to do some professional networking with Ms. Smith.

or:

You: I'm hoping Ms. Smith can answer a couple of quick questions for me.

REMEMBER TO NETWORK

As I said earlier, it can be an effective job search strategy to approach hiring managers from the perspective of a networker, rather than a job seeker. Except when you are answering an ad for a specific job opening, consider every hiring manager you speak with to be a networking contact rather than a direct source to a job. With this agenda in mind, you are no longer a job seeker looking for a handout, but a professional who is interested in learning more about the company and the industry.

In this case, you can refer to the research you did on the company as the reason for your telephone call. For example, try directing the conversation this way:

> You: "Hi, Mr. Moody, this is James Jobseeker. I'm following up on a letter I sent you last week about your company's acquisition of our local firm, HYCO. The newspaper article I read stated that you'd be hiring some new staff to expand the operations there, and I was wondering what the time frame is for this to occur?"

> Employer: "Well, we're going to be working on the HYCO situation throughout the year. You should call personnel if you are interested in working there."

> You: "Actually, I have some questions that I think you might be able to help me with, if you can give me just a moment. I wondered if you can tell me what type of staff you plan to move in to HYCO? Have you identified any specific needs?"

> This line of questioning gets at the idea of discerning the company's needs before presenting your strengths. Listen carefully as the hiring manager mentions the needs of the organization, then show how your strengths match those needs.

> You: "It sounds like my background in information systems may fit well with your plans to merge computer systems. In fact, I've done this before for SySTEM-EX when they bought out Kline-Fischer. I headed a team that came in and merged their two systems so that all the offices were integrated and linked. We managed to do a 5,000-unit system in only months, and we held it under budget, too. Can you suggest someone I might talk with at your company who might be able to tell me more about the information systems side of the transition? I'd like to find out more."

Here, the goal of your conversation is not to get a direct job offer, but to get the names of other people you can call to continue your networking. Each time you discuss your background and skills with these contacts, you are one step closer to landing the job offer you want. The very next person you meet could be the one who pops the question and offers you the job of your dreams.

This may sound like a roundabout way to search for a job, but it is actually one of the most effective and fastest ways to land a position. Each person you speak to will be aware that you are in the job market and will keep you in mind for upcoming positions. Cultivating a growing list of active job search connections is the best way to find a job fast and to land multiple offers.

Notice that you are not denying or hiding the fact that you are looking for a job. The trick is to let the employers know that you are in the job market, but you are not seeking a job directly from *them*. This way you are not a threat to their time.

Today's professionals are very open to networking with other professionals. In fact, as the workplace has become increasingly transient, the value of having a list of networking contacts has grown in value. You should have no trouble making a receptive connection.

Try networking not only with hiring managers, but with industry colleagues as well. Professionals at roughly the same professional level will see the networking relationship you establish as a two-way street: They put you in touch with important contacts and you do the same for them.

As your list of contacts spreads, with both colleagues and hiring managers, your chances of landing a job grows exponentially. Not only will you be conducting a thorough and goal-directed job search, but you will develop a list of solid contacts that will remain useful throughout the scope of your career.

POLISHING YOUR PHONE PRESENTATION

After all the work of writing and sending your cover letter and resume, don't blow your job chances by making a poor telephone presentation. Here are some suggestions to help you be your best on the phone:

- **Practice** Practice your presentation with a friend or loved one. Before you make the call, you should plan what you want to say, and polish it well. This way, your words will flow easily when the employer is on the line, even if your tongue tends to tie itself into knots under stress.

- **Listen attentively**   Remember that before you sell the employer on your skills, you should find out what skills he or she is looking for. This should be a *two-way conversation,* not an oral essay.

- **Be energetic**   Keep your voice level up and your energy level high. A quiet, monotonous voice can come across the telephone line as bored, tired, or uninterested.

TRACKING YOUR FOLLOW-UP

A busy job seeker can send out 10 to 20 letters a day or more. That's a lot of promises for follow-up phone calls! It is important that you keep careful track of the letters you've sent, so that you can manage your follow-up properly. You might try using a tracking sheet that looks something like this:

DAILY ACTION PLAN _____   **Date** / /

Company Name _____

Address_____

Telephone_____

Contact Name_____

Contact Title_____

Other Names_____

Advertised job / Referral / Targeted company / Other (circle one)

Date letter/Resume sent_____

Follow-up date_____

Follow-up results_____
_____
_____
_____

Next Required Action_____

You can print several tracking sheets on a page or set up a separate page for each contact. The choice is yours. Either way, tracking your follow-ups in writing helps keep you focused and on top of the commitments you made in your cover letter.

CHAPTER SUMMARY

In this chapter, you learned to make effective phone calls that follow up on the cover letters that you send to companies in your job search.

CHAPTER 17

Other Letters You'll Need in Your Job Search

In this chapter, you will receive quick tips that guide you through several types of letters you may be writing in the course of your job search, and you are given a sample of each type of letter you may encounter.

LETTERS YOU MAY NEED

As your job search continues and some of your early job leads begin to mature, you may find yourself having to write unfamiliar letters to handle new situations. In fact, if you are doing the job search correctly, you will at any one time have many job leads at various stages of development. In this case, you may find yourself becoming quite an accomplished letter writer. These letters might include:

- Networking letters
- Revival letters
- Follow-up letters (to phone calls)
- Acceptance letters

- Resignation letters
- Thank-you letters (after interviews and meetings)

Although most of this correspondence is quite brief and should not be difficult to write, you may find that a few quick tips come in handy as you begin crafting your prose.

THE NETWORKING LETTER

Networking letters are written specifically to draw upon your relationships with friends and colleagues to gather referrals to other companies or positions, *not* to ask for a job directly. These letters help you spread the word through your acquaintances that you are in the job market and hoping to expand your contacts in the field.

Tips for Networking Letters

- Be clear that you are not asking for a job, but for help in making new contacts.

- Include a brief overview of your background and skills, even if the person you are writing to is familiar with your work.

- Explain the type of position you desire and the career goals you have, while keeping the focus on helping your future employer rather than helping yourself.

- Don't get specific about your needs and obligations; leave off all requests regarding salary or workplace specifics.

- You may wish to ask for job search advice in your letter, such as, "Any ideas on companies that may be looking for someone like me?" or "Can you give my resume a quick glance and tell me if I seem to hit the nail on the head?"

March 19, 2000

Joan Powell
Head Reference Librarian
Mason Library
1624 Maple Avenue
Ellicott City, MD 21044
(410) 555-1212

Dear Ms. Powell,

Hello! I hope you are becoming acclimated to your new position at the Mason branch. Many of the patrons here at Liberty still ask for you and are always disappointed to hear you have left. Our monthly lunch meetings aren't the same without you, either. We hope you will come back to visit us soon.

Joan, I am also writing to you in hopes that you can be of assistance to me. You may know that the Liberty library has been making extensive cuts recently, and I am sorry to report that the children's resources have been cut dramatically. Because of this, I am looking for a position as children's librarian at another branch that has a more stable funding situation. I am hoping that your connections with the county might make you aware of a branch in need of an experienced children's librarian.

I have enjoyed my six years at Liberty very much, and am hoping to find a position with a similar emphasis on children's programming. As you know, Liberty earned an excellent reputation during my tenure for creative, high-quality event programs for children of all ages. I enjoyed fostering the community's good will and respect, and would like to take the skills I learned in this capacity to another position.

If you are able to refer me to any leads, I would appreciate it. I have enclosed my resume so you might have it on hand should something arise. I will call you later in the week to follow up.

Thanks for your help, Joan. I look forward to talking with you soon.

Yours Truly,

Sarah Peters

Sarah Peters

THE REVIVAL LETTER

These letters attempt to jump-start a stalled job search situation. Revival letters can be used when your first attempts at generating interest in your job candidacy have failed.

Tips for Revival Letters

- Don't be negative or accusatory. Be very careful not to sound like your feelings have been hurt.

- Express your continued enthusiasm for the position, if you think it may still be open.

- Even though this employer's interest in you does not seem strong, do promise that you will follow up your letter with a phone call, and then be true to your word.

Peter Blair
11978 Osceola Lane
Schenectady, NY 12302

May 13, 2000

Adolf Lekebusch
Customer Support Manager
Wray Laser Systems, Inc.
2131 Taft Street
Dunloggin, CO 31221

Dear Mr. Lekebusch,

On April 8, I sent a letter to your attention expressing my interest in joining your firm as a customer support representative. As of today's date, I have not received a response, and I am writing to you to reiterate my interest in bringing my skills to your organization.

During the past three years, I have gained progressively responsible experience as a customer support representative with Matrex, a manufacturer of high-volume copier equipment. In this time, I provided sales support to major commercial and institutional hires. I also worked extensively with government accounts, and feel that my knowledge in this area would enable me to hit the ground running at Wray Laser.

I have enclosed a second copy of my resume for your review. I would be happy to further outline my capabilities and learn more about Wray Laser Systems during a personal interview. I will call you early next week to see if we might schedule a time to meet. Or, I may be reached at (301) 555-1212, and by e-mail at PBLAIR@home.com.

Thank you for your consideration.

Sincerely,

Peter Blair

Peter Blair

THE FOLLOW-UP LETTER (AFTER TELEPHONE CONTACT)

If a hiring manager takes the time to talk with you by telephone, it is important to show your gratitude by sending a quick follow-up note. This doesn't have to be long-winded or fancy. Just follow some simple rules.

Tips for Follow-Up Letters

* Use this opportunity to remind the hiring manager of your skills as they relate to the position or the company.

* In your letter, refer to a comment the hiring manager made in the phone conversation. This will be flattering, and prove that you were listening.

* Express your continued interest in the position or the company.

* Even if you have already sent your resume recently, consider sending another with your follow-up letter. It never hurts to put your resume in a hiring manager's hands.

* This type of letter can be a bit less formal than the typical cover letter, since you have spoken with the recipient directly. Try to write a little warmth into the letter while preserving the professional tone.

Ward Brumble
1875 West 4th Street
Papillon, NE 68046

May 4, 2000

Klebe Marketing, Inc.
Lisa Jackson, Director
Account Services
354 N. 114th Ave.
Omaha, NE 68162

Dear Ms. Jackson,

Thank you for taking the time to speak with me by telephone yesterday. I enjoyed our conversation, and after talking with you, I have a much clearer understanding of your company's relocation process.

I was particularly intrigued by the comment you made regarding your expanded financial services operations at the new site. This information convinced me that my background in account services would fit well with your growing organization's needs. My experience as a credit representative has given me a broad background in everything from controlling delinquent accounts to scheduling account representative's field activities.

You also mentioned that your new offices will be using Excel and Word. I am proficient in both, and have taught Word to new hires on several occasions.

I realize that you will not be ready to conduct personal interviews for three to five weeks. At that time, I would enjoy meeting you so that we could continue our discussion of how my skills fit with your company's needs. I will call you again in a few weeks to see where you are in the process.

Meanwhile, I am enclosing a resume for your review. If you'd like to reach me, you can call me at home at (513) 555-1345.

Thanks again for talking with me!

Best Regards,

Ward Brumble

THE ACCEPTANCE LETTER

While you may have already accepted a job in person or by telephone, acceptance letters confirm your acceptance of a job offer by putting it in writing. These letters can be brief, but should take the opportunity to formalize the terms of the agreement if the company has not already done so on paper.

Tips for Acceptance Letters

- Express your gratitude for the job offer and your enthusiasm for joining the organization.
- Be specific about the terms of your agreement.
- If you have received a letter from your employer spelling out the terms of your employment, you may want to reiterate these terms in your acceptance letter and state that you agree with the terms as written.
- Clarify the date and time that you will report to work.

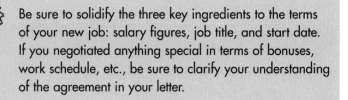

Be sure to solidify the three key ingredients to the terms of your new job: salary figures, job title, and start date. If you negotiated anything special in terms of bonuses, work schedule, etc., be sure to clarify your understanding of the agreement in your letter.

Carl Brandt
56 Overlook Court
Carrolton, NY 14788

May 2, 2000

Kevin Donovan
Director, Economic Development
Benham County Department of Development
343 High Street
Benham, OH 45212

Dear Mr. Donovan,

I would like to express my appreciation for your telephone call offering me the position of Development Specialist, Grade II at a starting salary of $44,146 per year. Please allow this letter to serve as my formal acceptance of your offer.

I am enthusiastic about joining the development team in Benham County. The people I met on my three interviews at your offices seemed to enjoy a solid team spirit and professional attitude. You and your staff have been very helpful and welcoming throughout the hiring process.

I will report to work on May 22 at 8:00 a.m. as we discussed. Thank you for the opportunity to join the team at Benham County. I look forward to seeing you soon.

Sincerely,

Carl Brandt

THE RESIGNATION LETTER

The current standard of business protocol is to offer at least two weeks' notice from your announcement of resignation to your date of departure. These letters can be brief, but they must be courteous. Be careful not to burn bridges, even if you are parting on unfriendly terms.

Tips for Resignation Letters

- Your letter may explain the reason for your departure, but this is not necessary.

- The more positive your note can be, the better. Why not compliment the boss' management style or the professional atmosphere of the company?

- You may want to communicate your wish to be helpful in the transition period, as other staff is assigned your duties.

THE THANK-YOU LETTER (AFTER AN INTERVIEW OR MEETING)

A thank-you letter must be written after each job interview, regardless of whether you are interested in the position. A timely letter of appreciation tells the potential employer that you have follow-through, initiative, and professional courtesy.

You must also write a note of appreciation for any other face-to-face meetings, such as a networking meeting with a target company or a personal meeting with a recruiter.

Ellen Thornton
18 North Justin Drive
Catonsville, VA 79045

June 16, 2000

Dean Takeno
Manager, Marketing Division
Photo-Lite Industries
2020 Norhurst Way North
Washington, DC 10018

Dear Mr. Takeno,

Please accept this letter as my formal resignation from Photo-Lite Industries. My final date of employment will be June 30, 2000.

The experience and knowledge gained during my seven years with Photo-Lite are something I am grateful for. During my tenure with the company, I have had the pleasure to work with some of the most professional and considerate managers in the business.

I'd like to express my sincere appreciation to you and the rest of the management team for your support and encouragement.

Best Regards,

Ellen Thornton

Ellen Thornton

Tips for Thank-you Letters

- Send the letter no later than two to three business days after the interview date.

- Be careful to spell all names correctly and to use exact titles. If you are unsure, call the company and ask.

- The trend has moved away from handwritten letters that appear more personal than professional. Thank-you letters should be typewritten, on white or ivory stationery that matches your cover letter and resume paper.

 Each letter in your job search campaign, from the earliest cover letters to the final acceptance letter, should match the others in professional tone and traditional styling.

- Make it unique: Mention particular comments that the interviewer made, and address specific needs of the organization.

- Don't forget to reiterate your interest in the company or the position. Interviewers and recruiters look for enthusiasm!

 Gather your thoughts about the meeting or interview and write a letter that reinforces the skills that seem to be of greatest importance. A quick reference to the things you discussed during the interview is all you need to refresh the hiring manager's memory.

Gert Willows
14 Devens Road
Swampscott, MO 29008

May 17, 2000

Barry Moses
Director, Marketing Division
Ryan Associates
7399 Wye Road
Thomkin, MO 29087

Dear Mr. Moses,

I enjoyed meeting with you yesterday to discuss the marketing manager position you have available in the Brokerton office. I was very impressed with the friendly, professional atmosphere at Ryan Associates, and am enthusiastic about Ryan Associates' growth and direction.

In our meeting, you discussed the importance of a new vision for the regional offices and a possible restructuring of the field organization. I'd like to reiterate that my tenure at my current company has prepared me well to manage such organizational changes. While here, I have successfully restructured our field divisions from 12 to 9 regions while increasing the capabilities of our service delivery. This has saved our office over $14M annually.

You also mentioned the importance of maintaining strong customer relationships. I agree that the ability to maintain and enhance customer connections is a vital part of any marketing program. Although I am no longer in the field, I believe it is essential to retain relationships with key customers and currently maintain close associations with the top management level of over 15 major accounts.

It was a pleasure to meet the management team at Ryan Associates, and I'd like to express my continued interest in the position. I'm enthusiastic about the possibilities, and I hope to hear from you by late next week as we discussed. In the meantime, enjoy your weekend vacation to Camelback!

Best Regards,

Gert Willows

Gert Willows

CHAPTER SUMMARY

In this chapter, you were given samples of various letters you may be writing during your job search campaign, and quick tips on how to write them effectively.

Samples of Ad Response Cover Letters

Lorrie Hilo
6723 Barry Lane
Madrid, Oklahoma 42509
(313) 555-9067

Ronald Bariman
Bariman Associates
789 Commerce Drive
Schenectady, NY 12303

July 12, 2000

Dear Mr. Bariman,

Your firm has been recommended to me as one that services a wide client base in the field of civil engineering. I am an experienced Civil Engineer who is planning to relocate to the Northeast and am pursuing positions with mid-size organizations.

Throughout my 15-year career, I have been responsible for the design and documentation on a wide variety of challenging projects. Earlier this month, for example, I completed a design on the stormwater drainage element of the Union Center Station project.

This project was praised by the *Union Economic Times*, in which the mayor was quoted as giving the design "two enthusiastic thumbs up." I like to think the precision and care that went into my design contributed to the wide acclaim the project has received.

If the enclosed resume is of interest to you, I would be happy to meet with you in person. I will be in Albany during the week of September 4, and could swing up to Schenectady to see you then. I will call you on Thursday or Friday to introduce myself and discuss the possibility of a meeting.

Sincerely,

Lorrie Hilo

Lorrie Hilo

enclosure

Brandon O'Shaughnessy
7690 Red Mark Lane
Brittany Hills, VA 67904
(404) 555-9730

June 4, 2000

Emilie Ericson
Ericson and Dowd, Inc.
58 Champion Circle
Montclair, NJ 89056

Dear Ms. Ericson,

Ian Matheson, a former candidate of yours who gave you a glowing recommendation, told me that you
have quite a bit of expertise assisting candidates who have executive sales experience.

As a corporate District Manager of Sales, I have had extensive involvement in sales, marketing, and
production interface. With an established record of initiating over $185 million in sales, my consistent
focus on growth and profitability is often noted and applauded.

My abilities in staff development and organizational management are also recognized as very strong, as
affirmed by the regional manager's comment that my "extensive ability to manage, prioritize, and motivate
others can be seen in the crackerjack sales force Mr. O'Shaughnessy has developed."

Should you have a client who would like to learn more about my executive sales background, the enclosed
resume highlights some of my other accomplishments. I would welcome the opportunity to discuss my
qualifications in more detail and will call you later in the week to see if we might arrange a time for a
personal meeting.

Thank you for your consideration.

Yours Truly,

Brandon O'Shaughnessy

enclosure

Marco Pangella
90 Venturado Court
Cincinnati, OH 45609
Mpang@AOL.com

August 1, 2000

Jerome Johnson
Johnson Associates
15 Market Place
Cincinnati, OH 45990

Dear Mr. Johnson,

I am requesting your assistance in my search for an administrative position in the health care field. I have a wide variety of skills, all of which further my dedication to success in the health care industry.

In addition to five years of experience as a Medical Receptionist, I also have worked extensively as a Medical Assistant and Billing Specialist with Mercy Medical Hospital. My varied background has given me a thorough knowledge of medical terminology, procedure codes, computerized office systems, and dealing courteously and effectively with patients and medical personnel.

I would like to continue working in the tri-state area, and will consider positions in northern Kentucky and western Indiana. I would appreciate an opportunity to meet with you to discuss my credentials in more detail and will call you early next week to see if we can arrange a convenient meeting time.

If you would like to contact me, you may reach me at home at (513) 555-8960 or at work, (513) 555-9090 X399. Thank you for your time.

Sincerely,

Marco Pangella

enclosure

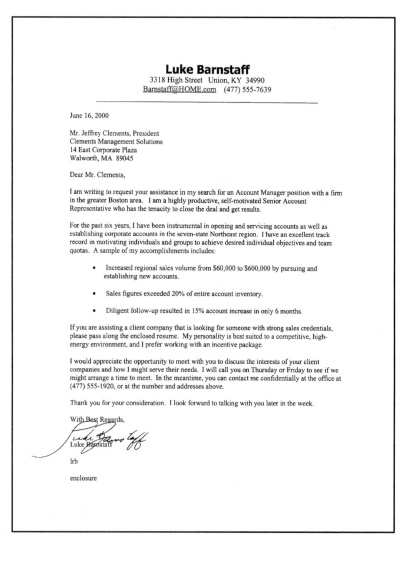

Luke Barnstaff
3318 High Street Union, KY 34990
Barnstaff@HOME.com   (477) 555-7639

June 16, 2000

Mr. Jeffrey Clements, President
Clements Management Solutions
14 East Corporate Plaza
Walworth, MA 89045

Dear Mr. Clements,

I am writing to request your assistance in my search for an Account Manager position with a firm in the greater Boston area. I am a highly productive, self-motivated Senior Account Representative who has the tenacity to close the deal and get results.

For the past six years, I have been instrumental in opening and servicing accounts as well as establishing corporate accounts in the seven-state Northeast region. I have an excellent track record in motivating individuals and groups to achieve desired individual objectives and team quotas. A sample of my accomplishments includes:

- Increased regional sales volume from $60,000 to $600,000 by pursuing and establishing new accounts.

- Sales figures exceeded 20% of entire account inventory.

- Diligent follow-up resulted in 15% account increase in only 6 months.

If you are assisting a client company that is looking for someone with strong sales credentials, please pass along the enclosed resume. My personality is best suited to a competitive, high-energy environment, and I prefer working with an incentive package.

I would appreciate the opportunity to meet with you to discuss the interests of your client companies and how I might serve their needs. I will call you on Thursday or Friday to see if we might arrange a time to meet. In the meantime, you can contact me confidentially at the office at (477) 555-1920, or at the number and addresses above.

Thank you for your consideration. I look forward to talking with you later in the week.

With Best Regards,

Luke Barnstaff

lrb

enclosure

Sally Campbell

1682 Colonial Way Canton, VT 56432
Scamp@Erols.com
(617)555-3443

August 27, 2000

Bruce Balmore
Right and Balmore, Inc.
47 First Street
Burlington, VT 58907

Dear Mr. Balmore,

Lisa Benesch, of your Sterling office, suggested I write to you in regard to potential opportunities with your client firms in and around Burlington.

For the past three years, I have been employed by Finex Microsystems as a Manager of Information Systems. As you may know, Finex will be relocating to Rochester, NY in June, and I chose not to follow the company to its new location. Therefore, I am looking to continue my success in MIS with another growing local organization.

Some of my qualifications include:

- Twelve years experience with corporate information systems; three in management, and four as Senior Programmer.

- Operation experience with several UNIX systems using UNIX System V operating software.

- Design and Implementation expertise for systems flows and operational details using IBM PC-XT System.

- Proven ability to improve information systems and networks by streamlining systems and improving methods of user training.

My compensation requirements are in the $90-$100K range. I have enclosed a resume, and would appreciate a time that we could sit down to discuss my qualifications in more detail. Ms. Benesch suggested that the best times to reach you are mid weekday mornings, so I will call you on Tuesday or Wednesday morning to see if we can set up a personal meeting date.

Thanks for your time. I look forward to talking with you soon.

Sincerely,

Sally Campbell

Sally Campbell

WILMA MAE DURNING

15 Rosewood Lane Mapleville, GA 67407
(716) 555-8066

June 1, 2000

Karen Waitcoat
19 Seems Blvd.
Lansing, GA 67431

Dear Ms. Waitcoat,

In the course of your search assignments, you may have a requirement for a dedicated and goal-oriented Quality Assurance Supervisor. I have 12 years experience in Quality Assurance, including seven years in various shift supervisory roles. My past four years have been with Vienna Biotech, where I was Quality Control Second Shift Supervisor, with a team of over ten technicians.

Of key importance to my success in the QA field has been my ability to handle day-to-day issues while planning for and implementing improved techniques and programs. I consistently focus on running a smooth operation while keeping a keen eye on efficiency and cost/production ratios.

The enclosed resume outlines my experience in greater detail. My geographic preferences are to stay in the southeast region, including Florida, Georgia, and the Carolinas, but I am willing to consider other locations. My salary requirements are in the $40,000 range.

Please let me know if my experience and skills are of interest to any of your client companies. If you would like to discuss my qualifications in more detail, I would enjoy meeting with you.

Please consider my inquiry confidential, and use my home telephone number to reach me. Thank you for your assistance.

Sincerely,

Wilma Mae Durning

Wilma Mae Durning

wmd

enclosure

Cooper Winetroff

1443 Woodmark Place
Cranston, NE 80017
(497) 555-8997

July 16, 2000

Ms. Clarissa Mann
Marks and Mann Consultants
65 Fieldstone Road
Connersville, NE 80018

Dear Ms. Mann,

The enclosed record of success in personnel administration may be of interest to you and your client companies.

I have over five years experience in:

- employee benefit administration

- pension plans

- dental, life, and disability insurance

My experience includes all facets of administration of the company benefits plan, including liaison with staff, management, and coverage providers.

I would appreciate your assistance in my search for a new position in personnel administration. My goal is to join a large, established organization in the local area, and eventually move up to a Benefits Manager or Human Resources Manager position.

Thank you for your consideration. You can reach me at the office at (497) 555-0911, or by email at cwinetroff@erols.com. Thank you for your consideration.

Yours Sincerely,

Cooper Winetroff

Samples of
Recruiter Cover Letters

Gigi Sheltraw
5788 Onward Court
Topsail, MI 54906

February 12, 2000

Mr. Mark Morosko, Director
Special Education Services
Wilhelmina Park School
12112 Chula Vista Drive
Farmington, MI 54770

Dear Mr. Morosko,

Your advertisement in the *Washington Post* for a Special Needs Services Director caught my eye. With nearly ten years experience in speech and language in school and private settings, I am well qualified for your position as outlined below.

YOUR REQUIREMENTS	MY QUALIFICATIONS
Six to ten years experience clinical Speech/Language	Nine years diverse experience as Speech/Language Clinician for multiple school districts. Masters Degree in Speech/Language Sciences, Iowa State College
Background in Special Needs	Three years with professional, private agency creating and implementing six special needs education programs adopted widely in local school systems.
	Received the Maxwell K. Mortensen award for my contributions in Special Education, 1996
Early Childhood Education	Bachelor's Degree in Early Childhood Education; Two years as Associate Director/Teacher of ToddleTime Preschool Center.
	Elected by parents as Teacher of the Year, 1999.

The enclosed resume summarizes my background and experience in more detail. I would appreciate the opportunity to meet with you to further discuss my qualifications and how I can best contribute to your needs. I will contact you some time in the next week to see if we might arrange a time to meet. Or, you may contact me at the above address or by phone at (604) 555-3748. I look forward to talking with you soon.

Sincerely,

Gigi Sheltraw

Gigi Sheltraw

Lesley Whisner
14 South Brad Street
Johnstown, IN 39086

June 16, 2000

Ms. Samantha Rose
Senior Marketing Manager
United World Products, Inc.

I am responding to your advertisement in the June 15 edition of the *Indianapolis Star*. I feel I am well qualified for the position of International Buyer, as my qualifications demonstrate:

YOU REQUIRE:

- A Bachelor's Degree
- Fluency in Spanish and Portugese
- Familiarity with Spanish Culture
- Retail Sales Experience
- Willingness to Travel

I OFFER:

- A Bachelor's Degree in Business from Kent State University
- Fluency in Spanish, Portugese, and English.
- Raised in Spanish-speaking household. Month-long annual family trips to Spain since childhood.
- Paid for college education by working nearly full-time in retail sales while attending school and achieving 3.7 G.P.A. Filled in for manager when needed. Attended to customers and balanced books.
- Enthusiastic about opportunity to travel.

I would appreciate the opportunity to meet with you and discuss how my qualifications could be guided to meet your needs. I will call you later in the week to see if we might arrange a time to meet.

Thank you for your consideration. I look forward to talking with you soon.

Best Regards,

Lesley Whisner

Lesley Whisner

J. Chase Kettering
5757 McIntosh Drive
Stanford, CA 94355

July 1, 2000

Ms. Marissa Woodrick, CFO
Filner-Hampton Corporation
43 Maineville-Foster Road
Maineville, CA 94450

RE: Controller position

Dear Ms. Woodrick,

I am writing to you in response to the above advertised position. I have attached my resume to address the requirements of the position as outlined in the *Maineville Times*.

I have sixteen years of progressively responsible experience in the management of corporate financial operations for successful, multi-state manufacturing companies and commercial operations.

My management expertise has encompassed all aspects of the financial and treasury functions, from Cost Accounting Manager to Chief Financial Officer. My track record includes the successful management of corporate real estate and general operations.

I have been a Certified Public Accountant for 12 years, and hold an M.B.A. in Finance. During the course of my career, I have traveled extensively throughout the United States and Europe, and would welcome further travel opportunities as your advertisement mentioned.

I would like to talk with you directly, and will call you within the week to see if we might arrange a time to discuss the position in person. You may also reach me at (415)555-3427 (home), or (415) 555-6901 (office). You are also welcome to contact me by email at JKETT@HOME.com. Thank you for your consideration.

Sincerely,

J. Chase Kettering
J. Chase Kettering

Lorraine Taylor

7 Burnette Court
West Chester, GA 78006
(670) 555-7896

June 7, 2000

Jose Gonzales
Vice President of Operations
Morris Business Products
14 Water Street
Clarkton, GA 77908

Dear Mr. Gonzales,

In response to Wednesday's advertisement in the *Georgia City-Sun*, I have enclosed my resume for your review. Your requirements for a Marketing Manager are an ideal match for my qualifications, as you can see from these outstanding accomplishments:

- Attained #2 ranking out of 57 regions after only 14 months.

- Achieved 162% of Quota for 1999.

- Reorganized sales agendas for company's two lowest profit districts. Both saw 60-70% net increases in the first year.

- Received the Globe Sales Award for Outstanding Performance, 1997, 1998, and 1999.

I have other areas of achievement that might be of interest to you. I will call you later this week to discuss your interview agenda for this position. You may also reach me at the above address and telephone number, or you may email me at lorrtay@AOL.com. Thank you for your consideration, and I look forward to talking with you soon.

Sincerely yours,

Lorraine Taylor

Lorraine Taylor

Enclosure

Sharon K. Tringle
89 Riderwood Road
Gleason, NM 89009
(789) 555-3759 (evening)
(789) 555 6899 (day)

February 4, 2000

Mr. Dean Donovan, Director
Harper County Department of Development
Harper County Administration Center
14 Main Street
Hughes, NM 89010

Re: Development Specialist Position

Dear Mr. Donovan,

Kristen Smith-Paulson, who works in the Harper County Auditor's office, suggested I write to you in response to the advertised position for Development Specialist. I am very enthusiastic about the position and am submitting my resume for your review.

My experience and expertise are an ideal match to the requirements you state.

You desire a knowledge of community development:

- As a community planner with Leberman, Inc. Architects and Engineers, I was directly involved in park planning for the 105-acre Keenen Park. I also worked extensively on the Glebe Road rerouting project.

You also are looking for someone who has experience dealing with government agencies:

- My current position with Leberman, Inc. has brought me into close contact with local government agencies, as well as numerous private developers.

I would like to sit down with you to discuss the other aspects of my background that fit with your needs. I will call you later in the week to see if we might find a time to meet. Thank you for your consideration.

Respectfully,

Sharon Tringle

Sharon Tringle

Samples of Traditional Cover Letters

Carolyn Smith
1212 Brett Boulevard
Columbus, IN 46990
Carolyns@Erols.com

April 10, 2000

Brandt Foster
Graphic Frenzy, Inc.
16 Commerce Way
Columbus, IN 46992

Dear Mr. Foster,

I am soon to be graduating from Purdue University with a Bachelor's degree in Graphic Arts. I have heard that your company produces cutting-edge graphics, and I would love to become a part of your creative staff.

I am a highly creative and innovative individual, and I possess strong written and verbal communication skills as well. I pride myself in being adept at translating a customer's needs and vision into a distinctive graphic design. My accomplishments include:

- Won the Washington Press Association's First Place Award for graphic art.

- Served as art editor for the largest campus publication at Purdue-Columbus, serving more than 10,000 students.

- Received highest honors at the Spring Fling Graphic Arts Show, held at Columbus's Florrie Hill Gallery.

I would appreciate the chance to meet with you to learn more about your state-of-the-art studio and to discuss how my skills might fit with your needs. I will call you next Monday or Tuesday to see if we might find a time to meet.

Thank you for your consideration.

Yours Truly,

Carolyn Smith

enclosure

Kiera Morgan
77 Taylor Lane
Chase, WY 70646

November 3, 2000

Mr. Sean Garrick, Director
Training and Development
Kroeger and Douglas
3466 Industry Way
Winston, TX 90883

Dear Mr. Garrick,

An article in the _Wyoming Gazette_ caught my eye at the mention of Kroeger Douglas. It cited your company's deal with Miro-word for 4,000 new computer systems by January 2002. It sounds like Kroeger-Douglas is growing at an incredible pace. Perhaps my experience as a Computer Trainer would be of interest to you during your company's tremendous expansion.

I have three years experience as a Computer Trainer with TransDyne, a mid-size textile manufacturer in Fresen, Wyoming. I am interested in relocating to the Winson area and am sending my resume for your review. My accomplishments include:

- Started and ran my own computer consulting business, specializing in webpage design. Netted $50,000 profit in first year.

- Trained staff on Microsoft Office, Lotus SmartSuite, accounting, small business packages, and statistical packages.

- Facilitated 5-day small-group workshop sessions for class sizes up to 20 members. These were scheduled bimonthly.

- Consistently receive the highest ratings on facilitation evaluations from class members and management.

I enjoy the challenge that computer training brings, and feel that my friendly demeanor and outgoing personality add to my students' learning experience.

I would like to discuss in more detail how my expertise might fit with your needs. I will call you on Thursday or Friday to see if we can arrange a time for a personal meeting. Or, you may reach me at the address listed above, or by calling (324) 555-8787. Thank you for your consideration.

Sincerely,

Kiera Morgan

Kiera Morgan

Murphy White
49 North Apple Drive
Fort Wallis, NJ 24409
Murphyw@AOL.com

May 14, 2000

Clemson Brummel
Brummel Association
64 Whitworth Way
Fort Wallis, NJ 24410

Dear Mr. Brummel,

Cultivating connections with local government and business leaders is not always an easy task, yet it is one with which I have much experience. As Deputy Director of Finance for a gubernatorial campaign, I developed a solid understanding of industries in the region and am on friendly terms with business leaders across the area.

I am currently interested in joining a non-profit association with a solid foundation and a clear mission such as Brummel enjoys. I feel that my background in soliciting funds from the business community locally and across the state could be of great benefit to Brummel, and I'd love to talk with you in person about how my skills might fit with your needs.

I can be reached at (779) 555-2059, or at the addresses above. I will call you later in the week if I haven't heard from you by then. I look forward to talking with you soon.

Sincerely Yours,

Murphy White

mew

enclosure

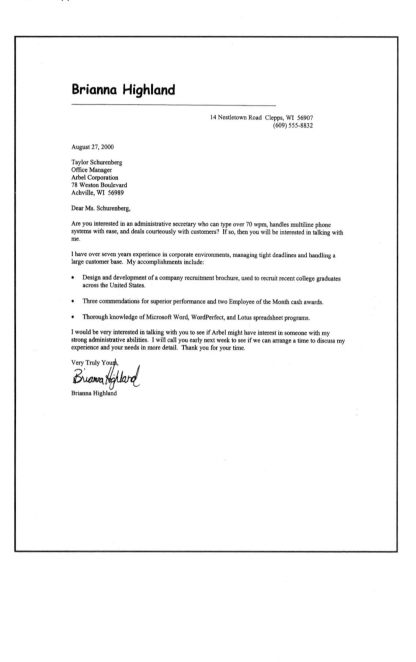

Brianna Highland

14 Nestletown Road Clepps, WI 56907
(609) 555-8832

August 27, 2000

Taylor Schurenberg
Office Manager
Arbel Corporation
78 Weston Boulevard
Achville, WI 56989

Dear Ms. Schurenberg,

Are you interested in an administrative secretary who can type over 70 wpm, handles multiline phone systems with ease, and deals courteously with customers? If so, then you will be interested in talking with me.

I have over seven years experience in corporate environments, managing tight deadlines and handling a large customer base. My accomplishments include:

- Design and development of a company recruitment brochure, used to recruit recent college graduates across the United States.

- Three commendations for superior performance and two Employee of the Month cash awards.

- Thorough knowledge of Microsoft Word, WordPerfect, and Lotus spreadsheet programs.

I would be very interested in talking with you to see if Arbel might have interest in someone with my strong administrative abilities. I will call you early next week to see if we can arrange a time to discuss my experience and your needs in more detail. Thank you for your time.

Very Truly Yours,

Brianna Highland